UNREAD BEST-SELLER

Captain G. A. Williams, O.A.
26 Alwyne Grove
Shipton Road, York, YO3 6RT
Tel: York 54439

UNREAD BEST-SELLER

REFLECTIONS ON THE OLD TESTAMENT
BY
MARY STOCKS

BRITISH BROADCASTING CORPORATION

Published by the
British Broadcasting Corporation
35 Marylebone High Street, London W.1.
First published 1967
Reprinted 1967
SBN: 563 07348 9
© Mary Stocks 1962, 1967

Printed in England by
Cox and Wyman Ltd
London, Reading and Fakenham

CONTENTS

Contents

FOREWORD

The talks which make up this little book represent random reflections on the Old Testament by a broadcaster who is neither a scholar nor a theologian. They were given 'live' between 1957 and 1964 in a BBC programme at 7.50 a.m. entitled *Lift Up Your Hearts*, which involved early rising and careful timing to make way for the weather report at 7.55. Thus they were heard, among others, by a number of inadvertent listeners, normally allergic to religious homilies but anxious to be tuned in to the weather report. Most of them were published at various times in the *Nursing Mirror*. But a number of listeners, both deliberate and inadvertent, have said that they would like to renew acquaintance with them – hence the present collected edition in which the talks have been arranged in a less random sequence for continuous reading. I have to thank the *Nursing Mirror* for permission to republish, the Reverend Adrian Carey of the BBC for his careful editing, and the BBC itself for letting me loose on the air to give expression to the excitement which I experienced from re-reading the Old Testament late in life, in the very readable *Everyman* edition.

Since these talks were given, events in the Middle East have made some of my comments irrelevant. The Jews can once again enter Jerusalem; but I think that we must still pray for its peace.

MARY STOCKS
July 1967

INTRODUCTORY

THE BOOK ITSELF

The longer I live the more I am convinced that the general title of these talks is justified. There are the number of Bibles one sees about. One may find one beside one's bed in a hotel bedroom; and one often gives away Bibles as scripture prizes in schools. I've often done it with a heavy heart because as I hand the book over, it seems to shout the answer to my question: why unread?

Wherever you open the volume, the pages don't look very inviting, since they are generally printed in double columns. It certainly looks like one book, instead of what E. M. Howse has described as a whole library of books selected from the literature of fifteen hundred years. There is a sameness about each page because the whole thing is broken up into 'verses' which seem to have little relevance to the subject matter. Why? Well, I must refer to E. M. Howse whose book, *The Lively Oracles*, is a wonderful help to an appreciation of the Bible. Howse says: 'In the days when the Bible was first being rendered into vernacular tongues, the majority of people were illiterate and the majority even of those who attempted to read were semi-literate. Hence they had to be taught to read and to memorize section by section. Practical English translators, therefore, established the custom of breaking paragraphs into numbered parts, a custom which is still a great help to reference, but a serious handicap to reading and understanding.'

It certainly is. But that is not the worst. Not long ago there lived a poetess (more popular in our day than Keats was in his) called Wilhelmina Stitch. Her poems appeared every week-day in prose form, so that until you read them (preferably aloud and rather fast) you could not tell that they were poems with rhyme and metre. Alas, the great songs and poems of the Old Testament are thus presented in the kind of old-fashioned Bibles which so many people acquire. Being translations from ancient Hebrew they have, of course, neither rhyme nor regular metre. But they have the thunder, the pathos, the rhythm, and the beauty of real poetry and they should be presented as such.

When Jerusalem was threatened by the King of Assyria the Jews
sang this song:

> He shall not come into this city,
> Nor shoot an arrow there,
> Nor come before it with shield,
> Nor cast a mound against it.
> By the way that he came, by the same shall he return,
> And shall not come into this city, saith the LORD.

A bit savage – yet when I read it in College Chapel on one of
those crucial days when the Germans were battering at Stalingrad, I
found it very satisfying.

And all through our own troubled times the Bible seemed able so
perfectly to fit the words to the occasion. Even Sir Winston Churchill
could not have improved on the words the prophet Joel gave us for
the morning of D-Day:

> Multitudes, multitudes in the valley of decision:
> For the day of the LORD is near in the valley of decision.

During one of the blackest weeks of the war in 1940 I went to
Morning Service in Christ Church Cathedral, at Oxford. The lesson
for the day was the Song of Deborah, from *The Book of Judges*. It
records the battle of Megiddo when Israel stood up, 'a remnant
against the mighty.'

> Then fought the kings of Canaan,
> In Taanach by the waters of Megiddo;
> Gain of money took they none
> They fought from heaven;
> The stars in their courses fought against Sisera . . .

Just in front of me was a young serviceman with a lady I took to be
his mother. He was obviously an unaccustomed churchgoer. The
Song was beautifully read by a layman and, as he ended, the young
man turned to his mother and said quite loudly, because he couldn't
help it, 'Splendid.'

People are not often provoked to behave like that in Church. But
there are lines in the Bible which, coming suddenly right at one,
might provoke that sort of outburst – for instance:

> I saw an angel standing in the sun.

Splendid! And if some of the old Hebrew songs are a bit savage, some have moments of great sensitivity and tenderness. For example, the most familiar of them all, David's lament over Saul and Jonathan. Yes, over Saul who had three times tried to murder him!

> Saul and Jonathan were lovely and pleasant in their lives,
> And in their death they were not divided:
> They were swifter than eagles,
> They were stronger than lions.
> Ye daughters of Israel, weep over Saul,
> Who clothed you in scarlet, with other delights,
> Who put on ornaments of gold upon your apparel.
> How are the mighty fallen in the midst of the battle!
> O Jonathan, thou wast slain in thine high places.
> I am distressed for thee my brother Jonathan:
> Very pleasant hast thou been unto me:
> Thy love to me was wonderful,
> Passing the love of women.
> How are the mighty fallen,
> And the weapons of war perished!

But whether savage or tender, whether they sing or thunder, with the exception of *The Song of Solomon*, one thread runs through all of these old poems, and that is an overwhelming consciousness of the responsibility of man to God and of God to man.

I know that some of my readers are quite happy with their old familiar Bibles and like them just the way they are. But I do hope that instead of writing to tell me so, they will think of all those – especially young people – who don't read the Bible because they don't like the look of it, and therefore don't know what they miss.

THE MORAL LAW

So many people have Bibles and so few people read them – and what they do miss! That's especially true of the Old Testament – partly, perhaps, because it is much longer than the New Testament – but mainly, I think, because many people who derive inspiration and guidance from the New Testament feel that, apart from being good literature and interesting history or myth as the case may be, the Old Testament has little to teach them about how to live the

good life in the twentieth century. It has its great moments of prophecy and poetry, of course – but much of it is pretty savage. The
God revealed in it is often a jealous tribal God, a lawgiver and a
judge with strong views on the efficacy of punishment – certainly not
a God of love with all humanity in his care.

All that may be the truth, and nothing but the truth; but it's not
the whole truth. I'm not speaking as a biblical scholar or a theologian
– merely as what is called a 'general reader' – but I'm sure the Old
Testament, or at any rate a great deal of it, can be an inspiration to
us today. For we have here the literature and history of a people
who were dominated by what they conceived to be the moral law.
They often violated it and revolted against it, but when they did
they had an idea of what they were doing. They didn't persuade
themselves that there was no such thing. And that was because they
believed and went on believing that the moral law was not a man-
made set of ideas, dependent on a particular social pattern at a particular time – as orthodox communists would have us believe – but
something outside themselves: a revelation of the will of a divine
power to whom they, as individuals, were responsible. Yes, and as a
nation responsible too. To such as had ears to hear, this power spoke
to men – sometimes through the prophets, but always through
men's conscience.

Today, though few of us accept the communist philosophy known
as material determinism, many of us (indeed some of the very best
people of our generation) think of the moral law, not as an absolute
responsibility laid on us by God, but as a matter of expediency at a
given moment. As Bertrand Russell said some years back in a television
interview: 'To love is wise; to hate is foolish.' Yes, indeed; how true.
But for our Old Testament writers there was more to it than that –
even though there were moments when they seemed to think it wise
to hate. Their tribal God existed and he was a supreme lawgiver. It
wasn't only a question of wisdom or foolishness, but of right and
wrong. They often broke the law, but they knew that it was there.
They lived in the light of it and sinned in the shadow of it. They were
a religious people, so I make no apology for talking about them in a
religious programme.

All the books of the Old Testament reflect this consciousness
except one, *The Song of Solomon*. I have always wondered how it

came to be included among the canonical scriptures, but I'm very glad it was, because it is a spring-song of pure lyrical ecstasy; a lovely greeting for the spring when the English climate produces a really worthy spring day. When it does we may read:

> Rise up, my love, my fair one, and come away.
> For, lo, the winter is past,
> The rain is over and gone;
> The flowers appear on the earth;
> The time of the singing of birds is come,
> And the voice of the turtle is heard in our land . . .

The turtle, let me remind you, is not the sort that city fathers make soup out of, but the turtle-dove – the bird that contributes the wood-wind to the orchestra of early morning bird-song in the spring.

OTTO MEN

Many years ago my husband and I were members of a holiday house-party. Eleanor Rathbone was our hostess and our fellow guests were two historians, Barbara and Lawrence Hammond, and (the oldest member of the party) Professor Samuel Alexander, whom William Temple once described as the greatest living English philosopher. He was, however, an Australian Jew, and with his massive head and long beard and wise old eyes he looked like a Hebrew patriarch straight out of the Old Testament.

One evening, as we sat round the fire, someone (I think it was Barbara Hammond) said, 'Professor Alexander, tell us what you think about religion.' And he began: 'I call myself an Otto-man,' he said. 'No, not a Turk but a follower of the theologian Otto, because I think that religion begins with a personal apprehension of what Otto calls "the Holy". It comes to many of us at times – it commands instinctive reverence and leads us to formulate a conception of deity.' I am quoting from a long memory; but he said much the same thing later in a BBC lecture – one of a series entitled 'Science and Religion', representing various points of view from Roman Catholicism to the agnosticism of Professor Malinowski.

Now, if you read Robert Browning's poem, *Bishop Blougram's Apology*, you will find that his cynical wine-bibbing old bishop, in conversation with an unbelieving journalist, refers to just this sort of experience. 'Just when we are safest,' he says –

> Just when we are safest, there's a sunset touch,
>> A fancy from a flower-bell, someone's death,
>> A chorus-ending from Euripides, –
>> And that's enough for fifty hopes and fears
>>> As old and new at once as Nature's self,
>> To rap and knock and enter in our soul,
> Take hands and dance there, a fantastic ring,
>> Round the ancient idol, on his base again, –
>> The grand Perhaps!

'Just when we are safest' – maybe after a nice reasonable mind-satisfying assurance that science has all the answers; when we have made up our minds that man can live quite happily, or quite happily enough, by bread alone.

The people of the Old Testament were never safe. Whether their experiences are recorded in myth or song or prophetic writing or fairy story or documented history, from generation to generation their story is the story of successive impacts by something which demanded reverence and inspired worship. It hit them in a variety of ways – in wind or fire, in the high places of the woods; sometimes through voices as articulate as those which told Joan of Arc to do the impossible. The conception of deity which those old Israelites evolved from such impacts took various forms and stimulated various patterns of behaviour. Sometimes it made them bloody-minded. Later it made them merciful. It might seem to reveal a tribal God – a national God – later a universal God. So we have in the Old Testament an incomparable record of such experience. And we know from it that they were never safe from this break-through, and their response to it was swift because they chose to interpret human life in religious terms. Nothing else satisfied them.

I say *they* were never safe from these disturbing onslaughts of the unseen. And I suspect that some of *us* are not quite as safe as we may choose to think we are.

THE LIVING PAST

I began this series of talks by saying that I had found a book called *The Lively Oracles* by Marshall Howse most helpful towards understanding the Bible. Since then I have found another, which a friend advised me to read – and how right she was. It is called *The Living World of the Bible* by Father Steve, translated from the French by Daphne Woodward. It is a rather expensive book, so the public libraries may have to be reminded of their duties to serious readers. It is expensive because it is full of fascinating photographs. Some are of historical (or pre-historical) remains – ancient stone gods or walls of long dead cities uncovered by digging. Some are of life today in Israel or Jordan, those two unreconciled nation-states created in our own time from the land of Palestine through which the river Jordan runs. Their inhabitants glower at one another (and sometimes shoot at one another) across the armistice line which ended – or halted – the Jewish-Arab war of 1948.

What this book with its photographs makes clear is what the traveller in these lands can see for himself if he is what one might call Bible-conscious. I mean the way the past lives with the present. Outwardly the thing is very simple. The ruins of Ahab's palace in Samaria are still there, so are the walls of Jericho – bits of them: indeed walls more ancient than the ones that were so conveniently howled down by the children of Israel under Joshua. The dynamic Israelis of today have substituted tractors and combine-harvesters for ploughshares and threshing-floors. Even east of Jordan buses and lorries are doing the work of donkeys and camels. But the past is still present. Shepherds guard mixed flocks of sheep and goats. There are still women at the well and fishermen on the Sea of Galilee. There are still nomads in the wilderness living in the same black low-pitched tents and dressed much as I imagine they dressed in all times past. You still go 'up' to Jerusalem through the sombre Judean hills, and when you get there the magic of the old walled city gets under your skin, even if, like the Jews of today, you can only gaze at its walls and domes from the look-out on Mount Zion.

But there is more to it than that – in this mingling of past and present, which of course you can see in most countries any day. We have in our own country both Stonehenge and London Airport, both pedlars and supermarkets. At a deeper level, what this book and its photographs help us to apprehend is the timelessness of this land and of the story which its changing and unchanging riches have to tell – and which the Bible records for us.

The writer of *Ecclesiastes* felt this long ago when he wrote:

The thing that hath been, it is that which shall be; and that which is done is that which shall be done: and there is no new thing under the sun. Is there any thing whereof it may be said, 'See this is new'? it hath been already of old time, which was before us.

I suppose this sense of timelessness is what is meant by apprehension of eternity. All through the Old Testament, its prophecies, its chronicles, its poems, its myths, we find human creatures seeking this apprehension. They found some key to it centuries ago when they sacrificed live sheep to a tribal god before the Ark of the Covenant – but they had a long way to go from there. Though not perhaps quite so far as the devotees of Baal in the sacred groves and high places of Samaria. I remember reading an article by the late Viscountess Rhondda in which she said that there are certain spots on the earth's surface which seem to exude some quality of holiness or spiritual significance. Palestine is one of them, perhaps because of all that has happened there.

PART ONE

PEOPLE OF THE BOOK

During their long history and down to our own day the Jews have time and again been conquered, massacred, led into captivity, and treated with varying degrees of savagery. Among the less savage of their conquerors was King Nebuchadnezzar, who finally destroyed the kingdom of Judah and evacuated its survivors to Babylon. There, as the one hundred and thirty-seventh Psalm tells us, they sat down and wept and declared that it was impossible to sing the songs of Zion in a strange land. Fortunately that was exactly what they did. For it was during their long exile in Babylon, under surprisingly civilized rulers, that Jewish scholars assembled their national records, wrote down their traditional stories and songs, and gathered together most of the material which has come to form our Old Testament: poetry, prophecy, mythology, history – and law. And from that collection there emerges first of all the tremendous figure of Moses, the great law-giver of Israel.

MOSES THE LAWGIVER

The story of Moses – how much history, how much mythology I wouldn't know – runs through four books of the Old Testament from his dramatic beginning among the bulrushes of the Nile, to his death on Mount Nebo within sight of the Promised Land. But I think you will see him most clearly as the great law-giver, in the last of those books, *Deuteronomy*, which is presented as his final charge to his people.

The late Maude Royden, who was a great preacher, though she had to preach outside her Church, once remarked that some of her most devout contemporaries seemed to have a queer standard of religious values. They would say almost in the same breath: thou shalt not kill, thou shalt not drink a cup of tea before Communion. You may get the same impression from reading the book of *Deuteronomy*. Some of its injunctions will seem trivial; some really brutal to men and indeed to animals. A 'stubborn and rebellious son', says the law of Moses, shall be brought by his parents to the elders, and all the men of his city shall stone him till he die. He who works on the Sabbath shall be put to death. Kill, kill, kill – there seems to be no reluctance to kill. And then – 'Thou shalt not wear a garment of diverse sorts, as of woollen and linen together.' So it goes on for page after page and then, at moments, up it soars to the uttermost heights of sublimity!

Ye shall not respect persons in judgment: but ye shall hear the small as well as the great. *Or*: The LORD your God is a great God . . . which regardeth not persons nor taketh reward: he doth execute the judgment of the fatherless and widow, and loveth the stranger, in giving him food and raiment. Love ye therefore the stranger: for ye were strangers in the land of Egypt. *Or*: This commandment which I command thee this day, it is not hidden from thee, neither is it far off. It is not in heaven, that thou shouldest say, 'Who shall go up for us to heaven, and bring it unto us, that we may hear it, and do it?' Neither is it beyond the sea, that thou shouldest say, 'Who shall go over the sea for us, and bring it unto us, that we may hear it, and do it?' But the word is very nigh unto thee, in thy mouth, and in thy heart, that thou mayest do it. *Or again*: Man doth not live by bread only, but by every word that proceedeth out of the mouth of the LORD doth man live.

Centuries later these words were quoted by a greater prophet. When reprimanded for breaking the Sabbath he remarked that the Sabbath was made for man, not man for the Sabbath, and told the story of a 'stubborn and rebellious son' without any suggestion that he merited stoning to death. So we too can be selective in our acceptance of Holy Writ, as we disentangle the gold from the dross. But let us do it with a *salaam* or, as the Hebrews would say, a *shalom* to Moses; when at the close of his lawgiving he looks out from Mount Nebo across the Jordan valley to the Judean hills where some day Jerusalem will be built, and so prepares himself for death and burial in an unknown grave.

As the ancient chronicler tells us, in concluding the book of *Deuteronomy*:

Moses was an hundred and twenty years old when he died: his eye was not dim, nor his natural force abated . . . And there arose not a prophet since in Israel like unto Moses whom the LORD knew face to face.

HER FINEST HOUR

Anyone familiar with the Middle East will know that its principal beast of burden is the donkey. Everywhere you see these engaging little animals padding along, sometimes so loaded with fuel or fodder as to look like walking haystacks. Chesterton wrote a poem about donkeys – and here are its last two verses:

> The tattered outlaw of the earth
> Of ancient crooked will;
> Starve, scourge, deride me: I am dumb,
> I keep my secret still.

> Fools! For I also had my hour;
> One far fierce hour and sweet:
> There was a shout about my ears,
> And palms before my feet.

If you visit Room 24 of the Victoria and Albert Museum you will see that 'hour' most beautifully commemorated by a fifteenth-century wood carver.

But now move back from Christ's ride into Jerusalem, back through the centuries to the time when the potent and prolific children of Israel were fighting their way into the Promised Land, to the discontent of those who already dwelt there. The Jordan Arabs today will understand their feelings. As the Moabites said, 'Now shall this company lick up all that are round about us'. What was to be done? Balak, King of Moab, had an idea. He sent for Balaam and asked him (for a suitable reward) to put a curse on the children of Israel. For it seems that Balaam was a recognized diviner. Today one hears stories of African witch-doctors who can make a man die by putting a curse on him. It seems that Balaam had such powers. He had, however, sufficient power of divination to ascertain that the very powerful God of Israel did not intend to have his chosen people cursed. So he said he would not do it – no, not for all the silver and gold in the King's house. The King raised his price: high office. No, Balaam still wouldn't. And then, for some reason that is not clear to me, he said he would and set off on his donkey to do the job. And suddenly the donkey (it was a lady donkey) found her way barred by an angel with a drawn sword. She stopped, and there ensued a battle of wills of the kind familiar to anyone who has had occasion to drive a donkey. Balaam told her to go on; she side-stepped into a field and he beat her. Then she got him into a narrow path between two vineyard walls and again the angel barred the way. So she squeezed herself against the wall and crushed Balaam's foot. Then she lay down under him and he lost his temper and beat her again. At which she said quite distinctly, 'What have I done unto thee, that thou hast smitten me these three times?' He does not seem to have been particularly surprised, for he merely replied that she had mocked him, and that if he had a sword handy he would have killed her. To which she answered, 'Am I not thine ass, upon which thou hast ridden ever since I was thine unto this day? was I ever wont to do so unto thee?' And Balaam said, 'Nay' – which I take to mean, 'No, of course I could not kill you; we have known each other too long'. At which point Balaam himself saw the angel, who reproached him for his treatment of the donkey and pointed out that she had in fact saved his life by stopping.

To make a short story shorter still, Balaam seems to have been somewhat shaken by this experience though he still shilly-shallied with King Balak, sometimes making as though he were going to pronounce a good curse with all the paraphernalia of altars and sacrifices, and then pronouncing such superbly phrased blessings as to convince us that though he might have been an unreliable diviner he was certainly a good poet.

In the end the whole thing petered out and, as the Bible says, 'Balaam rose up, and went and returned to his place: and Balak also went his way'.

But the hero (or rather heroine) of this strange tale is not Balaam but his donkey – so reasonable, so faithful, and above all so readily perceptive of divine presence. So, in spite of Chesterton, I count this as a donkey's finest hour.

THE FIRST BATTLE OF MEGIDDO

A few years ago I was driving from Mount Carmel down to the Sea of Galilee and I passed a signpost which pointed to Megiddo. Megiddo – to my generation the word recalls General Allenby's campaign when we drove the Turks from Palestine in 1918. But that wasn't the first battle of Megiddo and doubtless won't be the last, for Megiddo commands the fertile Valley of Jordan. It is a valuable strategic point. The first battle of Megiddo is recorded in the oldest part of the Old Testament: *The Book of Judges*; when the Israelites under Captain Barak fought for their promised land – inspired by Deborah, Prophetess and Judge. There they defeated Jabin King of Canaan and his Captain Sisera, who had nine hundred chariots of iron and had 'mightily oppressed them for twenty years'. Their victory is immortalized in the most stirring war song ever written: the Song of Deborah.

For Deborah was, I think, the Winston Churchill of her people. Without her inspiration that battle would never have been won. Very likely it would never have been fought. Israel was in a bad way – dispirited, unarmed, furtive. As the Song says:

> The highways were unoccupied
> And travellers walked through byways.
> The villages were unoccupied in Israel, they were unoccupied,
> Until that thou Deborah arose, thou arose a mother in Israel.
> They chose new gods;
> Then was war in the gates:
> Shield was not seen nor spear
> Among forty thousand in Israel.

Alas, I must leave out a lot for want of time.

> Tell of it, ye that ride on white asses,
> Ye that sit upon carpets,
> Ye too that but walk by the way.
> Far from the noise of archers, in the places of drawing water,
> There shall they rehearse the righteous acts of the Lord;
> The righteous acts of his governance in Israel.
> Then came down to the gates the people of the Lord.
> Awake, awake, Deborah;
> Awake, awake, utter a song:
> And lead thy captors captive, thou son of Abinoam.
> Then came down a remnant against the mighty,
> The people of the Lord came down for me against the enemy.

They didn't all come down.

By the watercourses of Reuben were there great searchings of heart.

Why satest thou among the sheepfolds?
To hear the bleatings of the flocks!
By the watercourses of Reuben were there great searchings of heart.

There were others who failed to come. But there were enough who did.

> The kings came; they fought;
> Then fought the kings of Canaan,
> In Taanach by the waters of Megiddo;
> Gain of money took they none!
> They fought from heaven,
> The stars in their courses fought against Sisera.
> The river Kishon swept them away,
> That ancient river the river Kishon.
> March on my soul with might. . . .

And then the song turns to its fierce dramatic end: the story of the beaten Sisera who left his chariot and fled on foot and begged for water at the tent of Jael the wife of Heber the Kenite – and was killed as he slept. And his mother waited for him in vain and cried:

> 'Why is his chariot so long in coming?
> Why tarry the wheels of his chariots?' . . .
> Her wise ladies answered her,
> Yea, she returned answer to herself,
> 'Surely they have found, they have divided the spoil?'

And the song ends in a burst of triumph:

> So let all thine enemies perish, O Lord:
> But let them that love him be as the sun when he goeth forth in his might.
> And the land had rest forty years.

Quite a time by twentieth-century standards!

Yes, it's a savage tale and I wish I could add that it belongs to an age more savage than our own. But the cold-blooded massacre of six million Jews in the twentieth century leaves one little chance. Nevertheless the men who fought the first battle of Megiddo (and the woman who inspired them) fought in the light of the noblest revelation of divine omnipotence that their world then knew:

They fought from heaven, and gain of money took they none.

EVERY MAN FOR HIMSELF

In *The Book of Judges* you are in a world where there are no nations, only tribes; and gods are not so much local as domestic. As the record has it:

> In those days there was no king in Israel: every man did that which was right in his own eyes.

Judges is a most interesting book. It contains some of the most dramatic stories of the Bible; Samson and Delilah, Gideon and his fleece, some of the most brutal stories of antiquity, as well as the greatest war song ever written, the Song of Deborah. What a song, what a woman! We've seen how strangely relevant it was to our emotional needs during the darkest hour of 1940. And, incidentally, it represents the oldest written source of the Old Testament.

The Book of Judges carries us back to the time when the Israelite tribes led by Joshua invaded the land of Canaan from the desert. They had to fight their way in, doubtless against some of their own kith and kin left behind when Joseph's family migrated to Egypt. They fought the Moabites and the Amalekites and the Midianites and the Ammonites and the Philistines. And they fought one another. Behind them was the desert and in front of them was the sea – and between sea and desert a fertile land flowing with milk and honey. And the tribe of Dan which had 'remained in ships' out of the way when Deborah's army was fighting for survival, certainly didn't 'remain in ships' when there was a chance of seizing 'a good land where there was no want of anything that is in the earth'. Moreover, it was a land occupied by 'a people that dwelt careless . . . quiet and secure and there was no magistrate in the land that might put them to shame in any way.' A people without allies. A sitting target!

The story of Dan's aggression begins with a young man named Micah who lived with his mother. She had accumulated a hoard of silver which Micah stole from her. However, he confessed, and she bore him no grudge, but explained that she had always meant it for him, so that he could melt it down and make a household god and set up a shrine. This he did; and in due course found a wandering Levite, whom he consecrated and set up as a sort of domestic chaplain with a stipend of ten shekels a year plus a suit of clothes and his food. All went well until the predatory sons of Dan came up from the south, six hundred of them armed 'with weapons of war'. They seduced Micah's priest by pointing out that it was better to be priest to a tribe than to one man, and they appropriated Micah's god and all the furnishings of his proprietary shrine. When he complained they merely said, 'What aileth thee?'

To which he replied – not unnaturally –

'Ye have taken away my gods which I made, and the priest . . . and what have I more? and what is this that ye say unto me, "What aileth thee?" '

But all he got was threats; so he went sadly back to his house (they had at least left him that) realizing that they were too strong for him.

And when they had conquered the people that were 'at quiet and secure' (though not as secure as they had thought) the Danites killed them all and established a city called Laish where they set up poor Micah's silver god, and recruited a bevy of priests to minister to it. And there they lived, I won't say happily ever after, but at any rate, 'until the day of the captivity of the land'.

That is the sort of thing that happens when 'every man does that which is right in his own eyes' and when there is no unifying and effective rule of law. Because then people devise all sorts of different moral codes to suit themselves – those who are strong and unscrupulous come out on top.

A SENSE OF VALUES

When the children of Israel entered their promised land, they had to deal with a number of native kings. These were mostly hostile – not unnaturally perhaps, since the Israelites came to possess *their* land. Many an Arab today would doubtless understand their feelings. When I was young the word 'king' suggested a male counterpart of Queen Victoria, who was then on the throne. In fact I suppose these kings were small tribal chieftains, but they were in one respect more kingly kings than the kind we know today, because they led their people in battle. This seems to have impressed the Israelites, because in due course they began to think that they too wanted a king. So they put it to Samuel the prophet, who did his best to discourage them by a really horrific description of what a king might be like. In fact he painted a vivid picture of a twentieth-century dictator. But no – they still wanted a king:

that we also may be like all the nations; and that our king may ... go out before us, and fight our battles.

So Samuel did his best, with the reluctant acquiescence of the Almighty, and selected Saul, who didn't do so badly until he became intermittently demented. After Saul they had a succession of kings, some good, some bad, until there ceased to be a kingdom for any Israelite to be king of. Today, kings are out of fashion and the children of Israel no longer want one.

But of all their kings, one lives in the memory not only of Israel but of the civilized world: King David. He had his faults – and it is to the credit of the Hebrew chroniclers that they are duly recorded. Not all historians are so honest. David is remembered by them, not only as a great soldier and ruler, but as a poet and a musician. And we still sing his psalms.

What makes him so great, judged even by the standards of the New Testament, is his generosity – his attitude to Saul who repeatedly tried to murder him – and his humanity. When his son Absalom behaved shockingly and led a revolt against him, he did not invoke the Mosaic law against 'stubborn and rebellious sons'. When the decisive battle was being fought out and he waited for news, all his thought was for Absalom. (Indeed he had given orders that none of his troops should harm Absalom – but one of them did.) And when successive messages came through to say that all was going well and the King's enemies were in retreat, all David could say was, 'Is the young man Absalom safe?' When he learned the bitter truth, we are told:

The king went up to his chamber over the gate, and wept: and as he went, thus he said, 'O my son Absalom, my son, my son Absalom! would God I had died for thee, O Absalom, my son, my son!'

Yes indeed – a great leader should doubtless be more impersonal. He should have been thinking of the safety of his kingdom rather than his own private grief.

Which reminds me of a poem by Robert Browning called *The Epistle*. It is the story of an Arab scholar who had met Lazarus many years after his experience of being raised from the dead. He writes to tell a colleague of this interesting encounter. Lazarus, he said, seemed a little mad. His judgement of what was and was not important, seemed to be all askew as a result of his brief sojourn in eternity.

> 'How, beast,' said I, 'this stolid carelessness
> Sufficeth thee, when Rome is on her march
> To stamp out like a little spark thy town,
> Thy tribe, thy crazy tale, and thee at once?'
> He merely looked with his large eyes on me.
> The man is apathetic, you deduce?
> Contrariwise, he loves both old and young,
> Able and weak, affects the very brutes
> And birds – how say I? flowers of the field –
> As a wise workman recognizes tools
> In a master's workshop, loving what they make.

The Arab scholar is left wondering. And when I read that poem I am left wondering, too.

WITCHCRAFT

All through the ages there have been human beings who sought contact with the dead, sometimes under pressure of personal bereavement, sometimes in a spirit of inquiry. Their demands have been met, sometimes by persons honestly convinced that they were in contact with the spirit world, sometimes by clever charlatans cashing in on personal distress. And all through the ages, both secular and ecclesiastical authorities have taken a dim view of such activities, penalizing witchcraft or fortune-telling, sometimes with great savagery often applied to the wrong persons.

So it was in the days of King Saul. In great distress of mind on the eve of defeat he flouted his own prohibition and asked his servants to find him 'a woman that hath a familiar spirit' or what we should now call a 'medium'. Here we have one of the most macabre and moving stories in all Old Testament history. They found one, at En-dor, and Saul went to her in disguise, with two of his servants. At first she feared that he might be an *agent provocateur* sent to trap her into breaking the law. But he was able to reassure her, and then he asked her to materialize the dead prophet Samuel who had been his early adviser and friend. She was able to do this. And when she saw the apparition she 'cried with a loud voice' and recognized the hooded stranger as Saul the King. Again he reassured her and asked her what she saw. Let the Bible tell its story:

The woman said unto Saul, 'I saw gods ascending out of the earth'. And he said unto her, 'What form is he of?' And she said, 'An old man cometh up; and he is covered with a mantle'. And Saul perceived that it was Samuel, and he stooped with his face to the ground, and bowed himself. And Samuel said to Saul, 'Why hast thou disquieted me, to bring me up?' And Saul answered, 'I am sore distressed; for the Philistines make war against me, and God is departed from me, and answereth me no more, neither by prophets, nor by dreams: therefore I have called thee, that thou mayest make known unto me what I shall do'. Then said Samuel, 'Wherefore then dost thou ask of me, seeing the LORD is departed from thee . . . for the LORD hath rent the kingdom out of thine hand . . . Moreover the LORD will also deliver Israel with thee into the hand of the Philistines: and tomorrow shalt thou and thy sons be with me . . .'

Then Saul fell straightway all along on the earth, and was sore afraid, because of the words of Samuel: and there was no strength in him; for he had eaten no bread all the day, nor all the night. And the woman came unto Saul, and saw that he was sore troubled, and said unto him, 'Behold, thine handmaid hath obeyed thy voice, and I have put my life in my hand, and have hearkened unto thy words which thou spakest unto me. Now therefore, I pray thee, hearken thou also unto the voice of thine handmaid, and let me set a morsel of bread before thee; and eat, that thou mayest have strength, when thou goest on thy way'. But he refused, and said, 'I will not eat'. But his servants, together with the woman, compelled him . . . So he arose from the earth, and sat upon the bed . . . and they did eat. Then they rose up, and went away that night.

You may remember that Saul fought his battle next day and was beaten and committed suicide to avoid being taken prisoner.

Sometimes when I have been listening to conflicting statements in a police court, a witness has told a story with some irrelevant detail which stamps it as a truthful record of what he has seen. I have always felt this about the story of Saul at En-dor. The description of his exhaustion after a crushing emotional experience, his refusal to eat — and the medium's down-to-earth solicitude for a man at the end of his tether (king or no king) — all suggest an eye-witness's record; perhaps one of his servants.

Whether what Saul and the medium saw was in truth a visitant from the spirit world, or a phantasm created by an acute state of emotional tension between the two participants, remains (to me at any rate) a mystery. But I am convinced that Saul was doing a very dangerous thing.

YOUTH AND AGE

When my husband returned from a visit to Germany shortly before the last world war, he told me that he had not met a single middle-aged man who liked what Hitler was doing – though in public they did not dare to say so. Of course, there were middle-aged men among the Nazi leaders and the business tycoons who financed them. But the main response seemed to be among the young men who marched, and sang, and gloried in the national prestige that Hitler seemed to give them – not to mention the power to bully people weaker than themselves.

I think those young men had their forerunners in the young men who were responsible, centuries ago, for the break-up of Solomon's kingdom.

Solomon had been a great king. There was a magnificence about his reign: his encouragement of art and architecture and commerce and foreign contacts – and indeed the tradition of his wisdom. He pursued a policy (not unknown in our own time) of focusing the loyalty of his people by showing them great public works and making them feel that they had a part in the splendour of the kingdom of David. The Queen of Sheba was speechless with wonder at what she saw when she paid a state visit; but in fact the people did not have a part in all this splendour – apart from paying for it with tribute and forced labour. And *that* they continued to do without any formidable sign of unrest.

However, even during Solomon's lifetime there were stirrings, and a revolutionary leader, Jeroboam, was biding his time. When Solomon died and the glamour faded, that leader returned from exile in Egypt, put himself at the head of the common people and presented their demands to Solomon's young son Rehoboam. They were not unreasonable demands:

'Thy father made our yoke grievous: now therefore make thou the grievous service of thy father, and his heavy yoke which he put upon us, lighter, and we will serve thee.'

Rehoboam asked for time to consider his answer: three days, he said. Then he called into counsel the old men who had worked for his father. What should he answer? The old men advised discretion. Be kind to the people:

'Speak good words to them and they will be thy servants for ever.'

They knew, I think, that there was a fund of loyalty to the house of David. That was not the advice the young King wanted. He sent for his own contemporaries – 'the young men that were brought up with him'. What, he asked, shall I say to the people? They said:

'Thus shalt thou say unto them, "My little finger shall be thicker than my father's loins. And now whereas my father did lade you with a heavy yoke, I will add to your yoke: my father hath chastised you with whips, but I will chastise you with scorpions." '

In other words: don't stand any nonsense from these underdogs, be firm with them; give 'em hell! That was the answer the common people got at the end of their three days. They replied with the defiant cry:

'What portion have we in David? neither have we inheritance in the son of Jesse: to your tents, O Israel: now see to thine own house, David.'

And when Rehoboam sent his leading revenue officer to extract tribute from them they stoned him to death.

So began the revolutionary civil war which ended in Solomon's son retaining a remnant of his kingdom, the hilly unfertile region of Judah – while Jeroboam held the larger and more fertile kingdom of Israel.

Let it not be suggested that youth is always more violent and headlong than age – though in this case it was indeed so. I can think of a more appropriate generalization. It is that a very glamorous king or leader may blind a people to the discontents of exploitation or servitude by giving them something to excite their imagination. But when the glamour is removed, mere force is no substitute. It has been tried so many times in history and so many times has failed.

In so many languages the cry has resounded through the ages: 'What portion have *we*? To your tents, O Israel!'

THE FIRST LADY MACBETH

I compare Jezebel with Lady Macbeth because she was the unscrupulous driving force of a vacillating husband; but she was a stronger woman than Lady Macbeth because, while Lady Macbeth ended her life as a demented, nervous wreck, Jezebel died like a queen.

In one respect she may be compared with Mary Queen of Scots, who came as a young princess from the elegant French court to live among the rugged Scots, and there incur the strictures of John Knox. So Jezebel, daughter of the King of Sidon, came from a busy international seaport to be the wife of King Ahab in the hill country of Samaria, there to incur the strictures of the prophet Elijah. For Jezebel worshipped heathen gods, while Ahab worshipped (or should have worshipped, and sometimes did) Jahweh, God of Israel. Of course, he shouldn't have married Jezebel; but men don't always choose their wives for religious reasons, and the forty-fifth Psalm, which is believed to describe her wedding, suggests that she was a most glamorous creature.

So the long duel between Jezebel and Elijah begins: between her gods and Elijah's God – between ambition and cruelty on the one hand, and on the other, the single-minded puritanical integrity of the prophet.

The most detailed story told about Jezebel concerns the affair of Naboth's vineyard. Naboth had a vineyard up against Ahab's palace and Ahab particularly wanted to buy it. Nowadays he would have acquired it by compulsory purchase as part of a town planning scheme; but property was more sacred in those days, and Naboth wouldn't sell. Here's what happened:

Ahab came into his house heavy and displeased ... And he laid him down upon his bed, and turned away his face, and would eat no bread. But Jezebel his wife came to him, and said unto him, 'Why is thy spirit so sad ... ?' And he said unto her, 'Because I spake unto Naboth, and said unto him, Give me thy vineyard for money; or else, if it please thee, I will give thee another vineyard for it: and he answered, "I will not give thee my vineyard"'. And Jezebel said unto him, 'Dost thou now govern the kingdom of Israel? arise, and eat bread, and let thine heart be merry: I will give thee the vineyard of Naboth'. So she wrote letters in Ahab's name, and sealed them with his seal, and sent the letters unto the elders and to the nobles that were in his city . . . saying, 'Proclaim a fast, and set Naboth on high among the people: and set two men, sons of Belial, before him, to bear witness against him, saying, "Thou didst blaspheme God and the king". And then carry him out, and stone him, that he may die.'

Which was done. And Elijah heard about it, and sought out Ahab and found him in his ill-gotten vineyard and prophesied a very dark end for him and his dynasty. As a result of which Ahab, we are told 'put sackcloth upon his flesh and fasted . . . and went softly'. But we are not told that Jezebel did anything of the sort.

And many years after Ahab's death Jezebel met her end – when Jehu, who had been one of Ahab's captains, rose in revolt against what was left of his dynasty. And we are told how Jezebel died – an old lady now, and left alone:

When Jehu was come to Jezreel, Jezebel heard of it; and she painted her face, and tired her head, and looked out at a window. And as Jehu entered in at the gate, she said, 'Had Zimri peace, who slew his master?' And he lifted up his face to the window, and said, 'Who is on my side? who?' And there looked out to him two or three eunuchs. And he said, 'Throw her down'. So they threw her down: and some of her blood was sprinkled on the wall, and on the horses: and he trode her under foot. And when he was come in, he did eat and drink, and said, 'Go, see now this cursed woman, and bury her: for she is a king's daughter.'

It was impossible even for that savage Jehu to forget that she *was* a king's daughter. She had dignity – but without righteousness dignity is not enough.

JEZEBEL'S HUSBAND

Everybody, whether he reads his Bible or not, has a mental picture of Jezebel; and the phrase 'a painted Jezebel' sums up all that many people know – namely that she used cosmetics at an advanced age. But what about Ahab? I think if a random sample of our fellow citizens were asked, 'What do you know about Ahab?' a majority would reply, 'He was the hero of Moby Dick'. A few would reply, 'Nothing at all'. And quite a number would reply, 'He was Jezebel's husband and the man who stole Naboth's vineyard'. And that discreditable affair is associated with one of those historical sayings which impress the memory because of their dramatic quality. When King Ahab, standing on the very ground he had so brutally annexed was suddenly confronted by the prophet Elijah, he said, 'Hast thou found me, O mine enemy?' I hope that future translators will leave it like that. I once heard someone telling this story on the air who rendered it, 'So you have tracked me down'. Not good!

Now it is true that in one sense Ahab *was* Jezebel's husband. She was 'bloody, bold and resolute.' He was bloody and bold, but less resolute. He had clearly married her for dynastic reasons – to strengthen commercial and cultural ties with the King of Tyre whose daughter she was, but she must have been very beautiful. She was not, of course, the only woman in his life. We are told that he had seventy sons in Samaria – not to mention daughters; and Jezebel could scarcely have been responsible for all of them. But she was chief wife, Queen Consort, although a foreigner and a worshipper of alien gods.

Now when Ahab faced Elijah on the site of his crime, Elijah was not the only enemy that found him. It was also his own conscience, and from that enemy he was never wholly free. It was the secret of his weakness. His kingdom of Israel was riddled with magic and witchcraft, omens and taboos and the worship of local gods in sacred groves and what are described as 'high places'.

Some years ago I was up in the far north of Israel by the head waters of the Jordan and I came upon a sort of glade – a little green space surrounded by very ancient trees. The place was eerie. I wondered if I had stumbled on one of those 'high places' for the worship of strange gods. I was not tempted to pay homage to Baal, but I was tempted to reflect that pagan local gods and natural magic represent the dawn of man's reverence for something beyond material phenomena.

Ahab, and Ahab's kingdom, stood between this primitive magic – patronized by Jezebel – and the conception of one god, Jahweh, who was conceived of as a just god although not yet as a merciful god. Ahab by his heredity and perhaps his own inner conviction was committed to serve Jahweh, but he was not always faithful to his commitment.

How in the end he lost his kingdom by listening to false prophets and ignoring the prophet of Jahweh is a long story. But the manner of his death in battle is a short one, and here it is straight from the Old Testament:

... A certain man drew a bow at a venture, and smote the king of Israel between the joints of the harness: wherefore he said unto the driver of his chariot, 'Turn thine hand, and carry me out of the host; for I am wounded'. And the battle increased that day: and the king was stayed up in his chariot against the Syrians, and died at even.

What matters in the light of any just standard of values is not so much how people die as how they live. But in history and mythology, and indeed sometimes in contemporary personal experience, people live badly and die well. Jezebel, who was cruel and unprincipled, died like a king's daughter. And I cannot withhold a *salaam* to Jezebel's husband, who died as a brave man leading a forlorn hope – 'stayed up in his chariot' through the day of battle until he 'died at even'.

LOCAL GODS

Local sentiment is very deep-rooted. Maybe it expresses the longing of mankind for an environment that is familiar and can conceivably be controlled, in a large surrounding world whose confines are not familiar and whose goings-on can't be controlled. There is a kind of mystique about localism which is very ancient.

When Jeroboam led the revolt against Rehoboam the son of Solomon and split the kingdom established by David, he became king of the greater part of it – the whole of the north. But Rehoboam held on to Judah with Jerusalem – the heart and centre of David's kingdom. And in Jerusalem was the temple – the holy place – the shrine of Jahweh, God of Israel, sometimes now called Jehovah. This produced an awkward problem for Jeroboam. He had the lion's share of the kingdom, the largest section and the most fertile; but Rehoboam had its God. And this is what, according to *The First Book of the Kings*, Jeroboam said in his heart:

Now shall the kingdom return to the house of David: if this people go up to do sacrifice in the house of the LORD at Jerusalem, then shall the heart of this people turn again unto their lord, even unto Rehoboam, king of Judah.

It was very awkward; whenever his people wanted anything, off they would go to Jerusalem, the capital of his rival, Rehoboam, to ask Jahweh for it. And thus a divided loyalty was set up. What to do about it? It seemed obvious – establish a god of his own – a local god. After all, Jahweh, away in Jerusalem, was a local god. So the story goes on:

> The king took counsel and made two calves of gold, and said unto them, 'It is too much for you to go up to Jerusalem: behold thy gods, O Israel, ...' And he set the one in Beth-el, and the other put he in Dan. And... the people went to worship before the one, even unto Dan ...

Nor did Jeroboam omit to furnish his local gods with a priesthood (not a very reputable one, I fear), a feast day, and all the paraphernalia that would be expected of a holy place.

But it was the beginning of trouble because an extremely high-powered holy man arrived from Judah and protested. I haven't time to record what happened – nor is there any need for me to do so because it is all written down in the thirteenth chapter of *The First Book of the Kings*. Jeroboam's local gods didn't survive, in many respects they weren't much good, whereas Jahweh at Jerusalem did. But no thanks to Rehoboam, who also fell for the lure of local gods in response, I suppose, to popular demand, and built 'high places, and images, and Asherim, on every high hill and under every green tree'.

And all that was very wrong and very silly, and very superstitious. But one has to remember that apart from what Jeroboam and Rehoboam did it was what people expected. There were Canaanite local gods all over the place. They were certainly demanding in the matter of sacrifice, possibly even human sacrifice, but they were profoundly satisfying. They helped, or so it was thought, to control local weather conditions, and promote fertility, and do all sorts of little things that the austere Jahweh away in Jerusalem couldn't be asked to do.

Who are we – twentieth century Christians – to take a censorious view of this primitive manifestation of localism, when all over Europe we still find local saints brooding over local shrines with special benefits available for those who visit them?

It was difficult for the subjects of Jeroboam to make contact with Jahweh – quite apart from the business of going all the way to Jerusalem. And anyway what did Jahweh want? Certainly not human sacrifices. Sheep and goats? Yes. But then arose prophets in Israel who declared that he did not really want burnt offerings at all – he wanted something quite different: something that was much more difficult to give. Hosea, for instance, said that he 'desired mercy and not sacrifice'. Mercy! – in that magic-ridden blood-stained land where you demanded an eye for an eye and a tooth for a tooth – and a few extra teeth if you could grab them.

Mercy and not sacrifice – so that was what Jahweh wanted. It was quite a new idea.

AN AFFLUENT SOCIETY

Writing of Isaiah, the greatest of the Hebrew prophets, Marshall Howse describes him as 'a man about town'. The earlier prophets, Amos, Hosea, and Micah, had been countrymen suspicious of cities. With Isaiah, he says, 'you enter the City of Jerusalem. You see it at its best and its worst, in worship and in wickedness . . . the whole range of its life, the fashions of women, the activities of court, the customs and manners of society'. Isaiah was living in Jerusalem, the centre of the kingdom of Judah, when the unspeakable Manasseh came to the throne – when, to quote Isaiah's own words:

Jerusalem is ruined, and Judah is fallen:
Because their tongue and their doings are against the LORD.

Isaiah doesn't mince words. He castigates the land-speculators who 'join house to house, and lay field to field'. He castigates revellers who drink all day until far into the night. 'And the harp and the viol, the tabret, and pipe, and wine, are in their feasts.' Which all sounds very much like the night-life of a modern city. And some of his bitterest castigation is reserved for young women who 'are haughty, and walk with stretched forth necks and wanton eyes, walking and mincing as they go, and making a tinkling with their feet.' He gives us a vivid picture of them:

... the bravery of their tinkling ornaments about their feet,
And their cauls, and their round tires like the moon,
The chains, and the bracelets, and the mufflers,
The bonnets, and the ornaments of the legs, and the headbands,
And the tablets, and the earrings,
The rings, and nose jewels,
The changeable suits of apparel, and the mantles,
And the wimples, and the crisping pins,
The glasses and the fine linen,
And the hoods, and the veils.

He prophesies an awful end to it all when the kingdom of Judah comes to grief:

Instead of sweet smell there shall be stink;
And instead of a girdle a rent;
And instead of well set hair baldness.

I wonder what the new translators will do with the 'tablets' and the 'glasses' and the 'round tires like the moon'? Clearly the mincing walk will suggest stiletto heels.

Now it may be that those 'daughters of Zion' with their wanton eyes were no better than they should be. That sort of thing goes with all-night drinking to the sound of music. But to many of us, 'changeable suits of apparel' and 'well set hair' and 'fine linen' don't sound necessarily wanton. In our own day many a respectable young woman walks with a mincing gait because high heels decreed by modern fashion prevent her from walking freely. Nor would one expect a dedicated male prophet to look with understanding upon the kind of clothes that quite respectable contemporary young women regard as likely to attract contemporary young men.

But it is clear that comparative affluence and the comparative (though very brief) security enjoyed by Judah during Isaiah's period did produce the less attractive symptoms of an affluent society with which we are familiar today. I'm sure those 'daughters of Zion' were tastelessly overdressed and very silly.

For all its vineyards, Israel today is a land free from alcoholism. And the typical daughter of Zion is a sunburnt young woman in shirt and shorts living the simple life on a *kibbutz*. But there comes into my mind the memory of a young woman being helped down the steep stone steps of Mount Zion: that holy place from which aged orthodox Jews murmur prayers as they look out over the Holy City they can no longer enter. And there is a notice reminding one that it is still holy. This young woman was screaming with laughter because her high heels and tight skirt made it difficult for her to negotiate the steps; and the young man who held her up clearly found her silliness rather attractive. Isaiah would have been shocked. Well – it's not the business of an elderly British Anglican to preach to the 'daughters of Zion', but if Israel becomes affluent (as I hope it will) I trust there will still be prophets to remind its young people of what so many of ours have forgotten – that reverence and good taste are not incompatible with prosperity.

THE BOOK OF THE LAW

In one of the saddest of the psalms, an exiled poet says, 'How shall we sing the Lord's song in a strange land?' In fact, that is just what they did; because adversity in exile threw the remnant of faithful Jews back on their own history, law, poetry, and tradition, and so the greater part of the Old Testament got written down and preserved. But for years they had written in secret and one section of what they wrote seems to have been hidden away in the ruined temple at Jerusalem where it remained – for how long we do not know, but both in *The Books of the Kings* and in *The Chronicles* we are told (with some variations) of its discovery. It was during the reign of Josiah, King of Judah, who at the age of eight had been set on the throne by a reform group of agrarian Jews. They had taken advantage of the chaos produced by the assassination of his disreputable father, King Amon, Manasseh's son, to make a clean sweep of idolatrous worship. Under their regime the prophets came into their own, and young Josiah grew up with due reverence for the old faith. At the age of twenty-six he decided to make a nation-wide appeal for subscriptions for the restoration of the ruined temple. The result was not encouraging. However, things went better when he instituted day-to-day collections in a chest outside the temple gates, and in due course 'masons and carpenters ... and also such as wrought iron and brass' set to work.

It was in the course of these operations that a book was unearthed which the high priest said he recognized as 'the book of the law given by Moses', none other than the very detailed code of religious and social behaviour which we find in Chapters 5 to 26 of *Deuteronomy*. It begins: 'Hear, O Israel, the statutes and judgments which I speak in your ears this day, that ye may learn them, and keep, and do them.' But it also contained sombre warning of what would happen if Israel did not learn them and keep them and do them. The nation would surely perish! This was disconcerting because it was certain that Israel had not obeyed the law – far from it. The high priest showed the book to a scribe called Shaphan, who took it and read it to the King who thereupon 'rent his clothes' because he too knew that Israel had richly deserved the fate indicated in the book.

Was it really as bad as that? They needed expert guidance. But strange to say they did not summon a conclave of priests or scribes – they sent for a prophetess named Huldah, wife of the keeper of the wardrobe, who, according to both versions of the story, 'dwelt in Jerusalem in the college'. (I wish we knew more about her and her college!) Alas, Huldah confirmed everybody's worst fears. All the curses indicated in the book, she said, shall fall upon Israel because they have burned incense to other gods. Only for Josiah did she indicate an escape clause. Because his heart was tender, and he had humbled himself before God, he would die in peace without seeing the evil days to come.

The King, however, did not give up all hope. He assembled the people and made them agree to a covenant binding them to keep the Law. That done he celebrated an outsize passover feast. Thousands of sheep and cattle were ritually slaughtered, roasted, and divided among the people. As the Bible says, 'There was no passover like to that kept in Israel from the days of Samuel the prophet.'

Alas, it did not lift the curse. Evil days and long captivity soon came to Israel. Nor did Josiah live to see it. But in one respect Huldah was wrong. Josiah was not 'gathered to his fathers in peace'. He involved himself in an unnecessary war with the King of Egypt and was killed in battle at Megiddo. Yet another battle of Megiddo! Deborah's army fought the first – Allenby's army fought the last. Let us hope it *was* the last. But an alternative rendering of Mount Megiddo is 'Armageddon'.

JEREMIAH THE COLLABORATOR

Twice at least in their long history the Jews have brought destruction on Jerusalem by refusing to let sleeping dogs lie. Neither Babylon nor Rome was brutally oppressive until provoked by nationalist diehards to hit back with savage force. But it is with Babylon that I am concerned today, because its rule gave rise to one of the earliest examples of wise collaboration against a tide of nationalism. Jeremiah was born into the kingdom of Judah at a time when it was horribly corrupt. When Nebuchadnezzar, King of Babylon, overran and subdued the kingdom, Jeremiah did not think it deserved to survive.

My people are found wicked men ... They are waxen fat, they shine: yea, they overpass the deeds of the wicked: ... and the right of the needy do they not judge.

Because of all this and more, said Jeremiah (who did not mince his words), they had evil things coming to them. Such strictures are never popular, and Jeremiah was not a popular prophet. Indeed his fellow prophets and the priests held that he was worthy of death for talking like that. It was the laity who saved him.

But there was more to come from Jeremiah, because having launched a searing attack on his own people he actually told them to come to terms with the enemy:

The nation and kingdom which will not serve the same Nebuchadnezzar the king of Babylon, ... that nation will I punish, saith the LORD ... Therefore hearken not ye to your prophets, nor to your diviners, nor to your dreamers, nor to your enchanters, nor to your sorcerers, which speak unto you, saying, Ye shall not serve the king of Babylon: for they prophesy a lie unto you, to remove you far from your land ... But the nations that bring their neck under the yoke of the king of Babylon, and serve him, those will I let remain still in their own land, saith the LORD.

To the Jews who had already gone to Babylon he said:

Build ye houses, and dwell in them ... And seek the peace of the city whither I have caused you to be carried away captives, and pray unto the LORD for it: for in the peace thereof shall ye have peace.

For himself he chose the hard way. He remained with the corrupt remnant of his nation in the doomed city of Jerusalem: doomed, because its people ignored his advice and rose in desperate revolt against Babylonian rule. He was there during the long siege which that revolt precipitated. He was imprisoned during the siege for causing alarm and despondency by advising surrender, for thus, said his accusers, 'he weakeneth the hands of the men of war that remain in this city'. However, he managed to survive when the siege ended in the total destruction of Jerusalem. Its few survivors insisted, against his advice, on going as refugees to Egypt. They took him with them; and what happened to him in Egypt is anybody's guess.

Yet he never doubted that in the end the power of Babylon would be broken, that Israel would be forgiven, and that her people would return to their land.

> For thus saith the Lord; ...
> 'Behold, I will bring them from the north country,
> And gather them from the coasts of the earth ...
> I will cause them to walk by the rivers of waters
> In a straight way, wherein they shall not stumble:
> For I am a father to Israel.'

They did, in fact, return as he prophesied, only to be re-conquered and re-exiled later. So let us accept his prophecy as foreshadowing the ingathering of the exiles by the new state of Israel in 1948, and hope that this time they have come home for good.

What he did not, perhaps, foresee was that history would repeat itself many centuries later when Judah was a Roman province and tolerably well governed. Once again the Jews neglected advice to 'render unto Caesar the things that are Caesar's'. Once again they revolted and brought on themselves nineteen centuries of exile and persecution. Of course, the advice to render unto Caesar the things that are Caesar's depends on Caesar and the quality of life which can be lived under his rule. But since on two occasions that advice was given with very great authority, we may, I think, assume that patriotism is not necessarily enough, and that national resistance to the death may not always be the right course – though on some desperate occasion it may be the only one.

THE PSALMS

It is sometimes suggested that the Psalms ought to be expurgated for use in Church because some of them are exceedingly bloodthirsty and call for vengeance on the enemies of Israel. I rather inclined to this view in my youth, but I have grown out of it. You see, I grew up in the late Victorian and Edwardian age when the idea of an exiled nation or captive nation didn't seem to fit human experience. And the poetry of the Psalms called out very little emotional response. Wars might happen and might involve changes of sovereignty; but they didn't produce great droves of wandering human beings – or mass massacres in gas ovens. And one couldn't imagine (or I couldn't) communities of exiles condemned to slave labour by their conquerors. Well – two world wars have changed all that. Now we know what the Psalms and much else in the Old Testament is a response to. So it all seems very much more alive. Take, for instance, *Psalm 137*, the song of all displaced persons. It is very familiar. It begins:

> By the rivers of Babylon, there we sat down, yea, we wept,
> When we remembered Zion.
> We hanged our harps
> Upon the willows in the midst thereof.
> For there they that carried us away captive required of us a song ...
> How shall we sing the LORD's song
> In a strange land?
> If I forget thee, O Jerusalem,
> Let my right hand forget her cunning.

And it ends:

> O daughter of Babylon, who art to be destroyed;
> Happy shall he be, that rewardeth thee
> As thou hast served us.
> Happy shall he be, that taketh
> And dasheth thy little ones against the stones.

That's a terrible ending. But I have taken the Bible version of the Psalm which says 'happy shall he be' instead of the Prayer Book version which says 'blessed shall he be'. Because it emphasizes what I want to say. 'Blessed' suggests commendation: it's a good thing to serve your oppressors as they have served you. And we know it isn't. But 'happy' doesn't suggest commendation. It states a fact. If you treat people like that, if you exile and enslave them, they will indeed be happy if and when they can get back on you. It's a terrible statement of cause and effect in human affairs – and we do well to remind ourselves of it.

REBIRTH OF A NATION

When the Jews went as exiles to Babylon they took their god with them. But he was not an image like the one that the Danites stole from Micah. Nor was he any longer a local god, because his temple at Jerusalem had been destroyed by the Babylonians. He was the embodiment of the faith of a people. Not yet a universal god as we conceive him today, but a national god who could survive in the hearts of men without a shrine, when the nation which had first apprehended him was a nation no longer – merely a company of exiles in a foreign land. Among the exiles was the prophet Ezekiel, and whilst in exile he saw visions and dreamed dreams – and he recorded his spiritual experiences in language of arresting imagery.

When I was a child we had an illustrated book called *The Story of the Bible*. I remember being fascinated by the picture of Ezekiel standing in the 'valley of dry bones', by which he symbolized the death of his nation and its rebirth in response to the divine call. There he was, standing in the dark ravine with overhanging rocks, on a carpet of horrible skeletons – the sort of picture that children find both horrific and irresistible.

The purveyors of horror comics today know how to cash in on this almost universal childish taste for the macabre. But, really, if you read Ezekiel's own account you need no picture to emphasize this aspect of it.

The hand of the LORD was upon me, and carried me out in the spirit of the LORD, and set me down in the midst of the valley which was full of bones, . . . and, behold, there were very many in the open valley; and, lo, they were very dry. And he said unto me, 'Son of man, can these bones live?' And I answered, 'O Lord GOD, thou knowest'. Again he said unto me, 'Prophesy upon these bones, and say unto them, "O ye dry bones, hear the word of the LORD. Thus saith the Lord GOD unto these bones; Behold, I will cause breath to enter into you, and ye shall live: and I will lay sinews upon you, and will bring up flesh upon you, and cover you with skin, and put breath in you, and ye shall live; and ye shall know that

I am the LORD."' So I prophesied as I was commanded: and as I prophesied, there was a noise, and behold a shaking, and the bones came together, bone to his bone. And when I beheld, lo, the sinews and the flesh came up upon them, and the skin covered them above: but there no breath in them. Then said he unto me, 'Prophesy unto the wind, prophesy, son of man, and say to the wind, "Thus saith the Lord GOD; Come from the four winds, O breath, and breathe upon these slain, that they may live"'. So I prophesied as he commanded me, and the breath came into them, and they lived, and stood up upon their feet, an exceeding great army. Then he said unto me, 'Son of man, these bones are the whole house of Israel: behold, they say, "Our bones are dried, and our hope is lost: we are clean cut off". Therefore prophesy and say unto them, "Thus saith the Lord GOD; Behold, O my people, I will open your graves, . . . and bring you into the land of Israel . . ."'

Many nations since then have been destroyed and recreated by faith in their own destiny; the Jewish nation among them – more than once. In our own time we have seen the resurgence of West Germany from chaos and penury, and from something like despair. Indeed, the whole of Western Europe bears witness to the swiftness with which national catastrophes can be made good and national hopes rekindled.

Only one line of Ezekiel's prophecy troubles me: 'They stood up upon their feet, an exceeding great army'. Must national resurgence always produce 'an exceeding great army'? It nearly always does.

PROBLEMS OF RECONSTRUCTION

The Jews didn't do so badly as exiles in Babylon. Like the Jewish communities in London or New York today, they kept their customs and wrote their books. And when the Persians conquered Babylon they got on even better, because the King of Persia allowed them to return to their homeland – and a number of them did. They had a hard time when they got there (like the Zionists of our own day) and the first thing they did was to start rebuilding the temple. And here – at the laying of its foundation stone – a strange scene occurred. It was clearly planned as a most inspiriting ceremony. As described in the book of *Ezra*:

When the builders laid the foundation of the temple of the LORD, they set the priests with their apparel with trumpets, and the Levites ... with cymbals ... And they sang together by course in praising and giving thanks unto the LORD; because he is good, for his mercy endureth for ever toward Israel.

(I suspect they were singing what we know as *Psalm 136.*) And, that done:

all the people shouted with a great shout, when they praised the LORD, because the foundation of the house of the LORD was laid.

And then the whole thing went wrong, because:

many of the priests and Levites and chief of the fathers, who were ancient men, that had seen the first house, when the foundation of this house was laid before their eyes, wept with a loud voice ...: so that the people could not discern the noise of the shout of joy from the noise of the weeping of the people.

As an ancient woman, how well I understand the feelings of those ancient men. Should there be any ceremony to launch the rebuilding of Piccadilly Circus, I shall stay away for fear of 'weeping with a loud voice' when I remember the old Circus, with hansom cabs jingling round the fountain and Dan Leno at the Pavilion.

But that was a minor trouble of these early Zionist resettlers. There was the problem of integration with the non-Jewish population already there. On this occasion the Jewish newcomers integrated all too much. It was reported to their great priestly leader Ezra that 'the people of Israel, and the priests and the Levites, have not separated themselves from the people of the lands, doing according to their abominations ... For they have taken of their daughters for themselves and for their sons'. Which report caused Ezra to rend his garments and pluck off the hair of his head and his beard. So he ordered a great inquest and those who had taken non-Jewish wives had to put them away and pay a ram for their trespass.

Nor was that the end of trouble with the local tribes. These greatly resented the influx of returning Jews and appealed by letter to the King of Persia, pointing out that a reconstructed Jerusalem would endanger his revenues since it would not pay 'toll, tribute and custom', also that it had been a rebellious city in the past – and so got itself destroyed – and was likely to be so again.

44

On receiving this letter, the King of Persia looked up his records, and finding that it was so, ordered the rebuilding to stop.

But the Jews too knew how to appeal to records. They pointed out to the King that one of his predecessors had in fact given them a mandate to build, and would the King please 'let there be search made in the king's treasure house, which is there at Babylon, whether it be so'. And search was made and it was so. The Jews were able to claim something like the Balfour Declaration of our own time. As a result the building was resumed – and, eventually, completed.

And there we must leave the matter; remembering only that history went on repeating itself; conquest and destruction, destruction and conflict. No peace for Jerusalem. But the queer thing about Jerusalem is that although it has been razed to the ground and rebuilt time and again, once you get inside its walls you feel that time and change have done very little to it, that it has gone on all the time, just the same. Perhaps because it *is* a very holy city.

A MIND TO WORK

Those of us who can remember the peaceful years before 1914 will realize how remote much of the Old Testament then seemed. Long ago we thought there *might* have been a time when whole cities were destroyed and whole nations led captive – but such things didn't happen nowadays. The idea of an exiled nation was unthinkable. It isn't unthinkable today, and some of the things we have seen and our friends have suffered bring those old stories to life, so that we can feel very near to Nehemiah, for instance, living in exile from the Holy City of his fathers, at a time when the only memory of Jerusalem was of a burned-out city in a distant land.

Nehemiah himself hadn't done so badly in exile. He had made friends with his captors and had moved into Persia as cup-bearer to the King. But when rumours reached him that those of his compatriots who had been gone back to Judah to pioneer the reconstruction were in a bad way, he was so sad that the King noticed it and asked what was the matter. 'Why should not my countenance be sad,' said Nehemiah, 'when the city, the place of my fathers' sepulchres, lieth waste, and the gates thereof are consumed with fire?' Then the King gave him leave to go back across the Jordan into Judah to see how the land lay – even supplied him with a bodyguard, because Jerusalem was surrounded by hostile tribesmen. Now let him tell his own story:

So I came to Jerusalem, and was there three days. And I arose in the night, I and some few men with me; neither told I any man what my God had put in my heart to do at Jerusalem. . . . And I went out by night by the gate of the valley, even before the dragon well, . . . and viewed the walls of Jerusalem, which were broken down, and the gates thereof were consumed with fire. Then I went on to the gate of the fountain and to the king's pool: but there was no place for the beast that was under me to pass . . . And the rulers knew not whither I went, or what I did; neither had I as yet told it to the Jews . . .

How clearly one can see him, stepping over the rubble, searching for familiar shapes – surely by moonlight. I thought of that scene some years ago when I prowled round the devastated centre of Berlin looking for a street where I used to stay with Jewish friends long since in exile. It just wasn't there.

Well, to make a long story short, Nehemiah rallied the Jews and said, 'Ye see the distress that we are in, how Jerusalem lieth waste, and the gates thereof are burned with fire: come, and let us build up the wall of Jerusalem'. And the people answered, '"Let us rise up and build." So built we the wall,' writes Nehemiah, 'and all the wall was joined together unto the half thereof; for the people had a mind to work'. And work they did. Nehemiah describes it all in great detail – each group doing its particular bit. One can see a new Jerusalem rising under their hands: the beams, the gates, the doors, the locks, the bars. And all the while they built under a barrage of mockery tand enmity from the surrounding hostile tribesmen; so that as they built, writes Nehemiah:

. . . everyone with one of his hands wrought in the work, and with the other hand held a weapon. For the builders, everyone had his sword girded by his side, and so builded . . . So we laboured in the work: and half of them held the spears from the rising of the morning till the stars appeared.

It's a grand story – and yet a sad one. Their work didn't last. How many times has Jerusalem been pulled down and built since then! 'O Jerusalem, Jerusalem, thou that killest the prophets, and stonest them which are sent into thee . . .' And now once more a great new city of Jerusalem is being built up outside the old walls by a later generation of returning exiles – and still its builders have to build with one hand on the work while the other holds the weapon. Jerusalem hasn't yet found peace. Perhaps it doesn't deserve to.

MORTGAGES AND EXPENSE ALLOWANCES

The reconstruction of a nation after defeat, or a city after devastation, is bound to throw up economic problems. So Nehemiah found when he set himself to the task as Governor of Judah after the return of the exiles from Persia and Babylon.

Rebuilding Jerusalem while holding off hostile tribesmen at spear's length wasn't an easy job for Nehemiah, though it was a comparatively straightforward one. But governing a surrounding territory with a mixed population was another matter. It was a mixed population of Jews with widely differing experiences and loyalties. Some were exiles from Babylon who had returned with Nehemiah to recolonize the homeland. They were the *élite* who had done a lot of work on the history and religion of their people while in exile. Some had remained behind, living under a Babylonian governor at a very low standard of life in the conquered province. Some were ready to co-operate with the returning exiles – some were resentful.

Here then was one of Nehemiah's problems:

There was a great cry of the people and of their wives against their brethren the Jews. For there were that said, 'We, our sons, and our daughters, are many: therefore we take up corn for them, that we may eat, and live.' Some also there were that said, 'We have mortgaged our lands, vineyards, and houses, that we might buy corn, because of the dearth'. There were also that said, 'We have borrowed money for the king's tribute, and that upon our lands and vineyards. Yet now our flesh is as the flesh of our brethren, our children as their children: and, lo, we bring into bondage our sons and our daughters to be servants, . . . neither is it in our power to redeem them; for other men have our lands and vineyards.'

Nehemiah wasn't going to tolerate such goings-on. He accused the nobles and rulers of usury, and addressed an assembly in very strong terms:

'We, after our ability have redeemed our brethren the Jews, which were sold unto the heathen; and will ye even sell your brethren? or shall they be sold unto us?'

That silenced them. But it did not silence him. He went on – ordering them to 'leave off this usury' and restore to the complainants 'their lands, their vineyards, their oliveyards, and their houses', also to forgo (and this transaction I find difficult to understand) 'the hundredth part of the money, and of the corn, the wine, and the oil, that ye exact of them'. I suppose he was telling them to reduce their rents – but only, it seems, by one per cent. However, they all solemnly promised that they would, and there was no more nonsense of that sort, at least so far as we know.

But Nehemiah had put himself in a strong moral position as governor, by forgoing the emoluments of office. He was able to point out that former governors of Judah were 'chargeable unto the people, and had taken of them bread and wine, at the rate of forty shekels of silver daily; yea, even their servants lorded it over the people: but so did not I because of the fear of God'. Indeed, he employed his own servants on public work and entertained at his own expense. There was, in fact, quite a lot of public entertaining – as he says:

'There were at my table an hundred and fifty of the Jews and rulers, beside those that came unto us from among the heathen that are about us. Now that which was prepared for me daily was one ox and six choice sheep; also fowls were prepared for me, and once in ten days store of all sorts of wine: yet for all this required not I the bread of the governor.'

He ends his explanation somewhat sanctimoniously:

'Think upon me, my God, for good, according to all that I have done for this people.'

But let us not compare this prayer with one prayed centuries later by a Pharisee in the temple – for Nehemiah really had done a remarkable job of reconstruction and good government, and had achieved home rule for his people with the friendly co-operation of the imperial power of Persia.

But doesn't it all go to show that there is really almost no such thing as a modern problem – not even the expense allowance racket!

When people talk about the Old Testament as though it were an archaic story of a vanished world, it shows that they haven't read it.

PART TWO

MORAL TALES

In the *Everyman* edition of the Bible, four books are grouped under the title: *Homiletic Narratives*, which simply means moral tales: *Ruth*, *Esther*, *Judith*, and *Tobit*. I am not sure that some of them are all that moral – *Judith* in particular; at any rate if you believe that 'patriotism is not enough'. If it is, then Judith gets away with it because she was nothing if not patriotic and prepared to exploit her sex-appeal in the interest of her race. So indeed was Esther who, as we shall see, showed supreme capacity for what might be called male-management by swooning at just the right moment. Of course she showed much else – intelligent initiative and cool courage, and is rightly venerated as a heroine in the feast of Purim. She did indeed avert a pogrom which would have been possibly less well-organized, but certainly no less brutal, than the one carried through by the Germans in 1944.

But *The Book of Esther* contains another heroine who has no annual feast and makes only a momentary appearance in the pages of history. Yet I have always had an affection for her because she refused to exploit her own sex-appeal, or rather to let it be exploited by others. I mean Queen Vashti.

QUEEN VASHTI

Vashti was the wife of King Ahasuerus of Persia, better known to history as Xerxes, who ruled in the fifth century B.C. The Bible tells us that he 'reigned, from India even unto Ethiopia, over an hundred and seven and twenty provinces . . .'

Now it came to pass that, in the third year of his reign, he made a feast unto all his princes and his servants; the power of Persia and Media, the nobles and princes of the provinces, being before him: when he shewed the riches of his glorious kingdom and the honour of his excellent majesty.

This durbar – for so one might describe it – continued for a hundred and eighty days and concluded with a gigantic feast in the court of the palace garden, which was decorated for the occasion with 'white, green, and blue hangings, fastened with cords of fine linen and purple to silver rings and pillars of marble: the beds (on which, presumably, the guests reclined Roman fashion) were of gold and silver, upon a pavement of red, and blue, and white, and black marble'. And the guests were given 'royal wine in abundance' in vessels of gold.

But though the invitations were issued very freely 'both unto great and small', it seems that ladies were not present, since we are told that the Queen had a separate party for them in her own quarters. And a good thing too! Because the King's party clearly developed into a drunken orgy. When they had been at it for seven days we are told that 'the heart of the King was merry with wine'; and I have little doubt that other hearts were merry too; for what can you expect if wine is freely on tap for seven consecutive days? At which point the King sent his chamberlains to fetch Queen Vashti wearing her royal crown, in order that the guests might admire her beauty. You can imagine the sort of conversation that led up to this request. Under the circumstances she (very rightly, I think) refused to come. And that was her undoing. The King was furious and 'his anger burned in him'.

Nor was that the end – because 'wise men, which knew the times' (I gather from the text that they were legal luminaries), feared a disastrous repercussion. After all, everybody had either seen or would have heard of the incident. What if the 'ladies of Persia and Media' should be inspired to follow the Queen's example?

They therefore urged the King first to depose Vashti – that of course was Esther's opportunity – but, further, to write into the unalterable laws of the Medes and Persians a clause requiring that all wives shall obey their husbands.

So that was the end of Vashti. What became of her? We shall never know. I should like to think that she was pensioned off like Henry VIII's fourth wife and allowed to live quietly in the country. Somehow I fear not. Thus she steps suddenly on to the stage of history, makes her one defiant gesture, and disappears into the wings. Hail and farewell, Queen Vashti – and *shalom*.

A POGROM AVERTED

When I first read *The Book of Esther*, being very young, the story that captured my imagination was that of Vashti, the defiant wife, rather than that of Esther the Jewess. This was because the women's suffrage movement was a passionate preoccupation whereas militant anti-semitism seemed to have no relevance to the world in which I then lived. And when Vashti was deposed and disappeared from view and the King then assembled a concourse of 'fair young virgins' from among whom, in due course, Esther was selected as Queen Consort, I remember my feeling that Esther was a scheming social climber who had exploited her sex appeal to supplant a good feminist. It is easier today to understand her position – in fact she acted with great courage in a good cause.

Esther was a Jew and there were very many Jews living peaceably under Persian rule which at that time covered the whole Middle East. She was an orphan, who had been adopted by her cousin Mordecai who had some status at the King's Palace. Mordecai was able to manoeuvre Esther into her favoured position without letting it be known that she *was* a Jew. But Mordecai seems to have fallen out with the King's newly installed favourite, Haman. And Haman, who knew that Mordecai was a Jew, determined on a large-scale revenge – no less than what in our own time Hitler described as a 'final solution' of the Jewish problem. He said to the King:

'There is a certain people scattered abroad and dispersed among the people in all the provinces of thy kingdom; and their laws are diverse from all people... If it please the king, let it be written that they may be destroyed.'

It *did* please the King, and the order went out for a general extermination of the Jews, men, women and children on the thirteenth day of the twelfth month.

There was no time to lose. Mordecai got in touch with Esther and urged her to use her influence with the King. She told him, what everyone knew, that the penalty for entering the King's inner court without being summoned was death – unless the King was moved to hold out his golden sceptre to the intruder. 'And I,' said Esther, 'have not been summoned to come in unto the king these thirty days.' Mordecai reminded Esther that the risk was worth taking, for if nothing was done they would all be killed anyway. She said, 'Go, gather together all the Jews, and fast ye for me: so will I go in unto the king . . . and if I perish, I perish.'

The story of her encounter is told most dramatically, in a later supplement to the Hebrew *Book of Esther*:

And being gloriously adorned, after she had called upon God, who is the beholder and saviour of all things, she took two maids with her: and on the one she leaned, as carrying herself daintily; and the other followed, bearing up her train. And she was ruddy through the perfection of her beauty, and her countenance was cheerful and very amiable: but her heart was in anguish for fear. Then having passed through all the doors, she stood before the king . . . Then lifting up his countenance that shone with majesty, he looked very fiercely upon her: and the queen fell down, and was pale, and fainted.

Then (says the chronicler) God changed the spirit of the King into mildness. Well – it may have been a spiritual visitation. But the young woman, so beautiful, so frail, and fainting at the right moment, got all she wanted and what she wanted was the salvation of her people and their descendants from that day to this. But alas – she wanted something else and that was a terrible revenge. There was a lot of killing by Jews of non-Jews, and Esther demanded that the ten sons of Haman should be hanged.

So it goes on through history. Atrocity and counter-atrocity. How long, O Lord, how long?

AN INCURABLE OPTIMIST

The book of *Tobit*, unlike that of *Judith*, *is* a moral tale. But it is also a fairy tale complete with demon king. The fairy tale concerns the journey of young Tobias, sent by his father Tobit to collect some money. He was accompanied by a hired servant, who turned out to be an archangel in disguise, and whose magic enabled Tobias to woo and win a young woman who was plagued by a jealous demon lover called Asmodeus. But, thanks to the archangel, Asmodeus was suitably dealt with. This fascinating story will be familiar to many listeners as the subject of James Bridie's play *Tobias and the Angel*. I want now to concentrate on the domestic life of father Tobit and his wife Anna. It is so vividly described in the Apocrypha text that one comes to know them, domestic tiffs and all, as one might know a kindly old couple in the next street in an age when refugees and persecuted minorities have become familiar facts of life.

The Tobits were indeed Jewish refugees who, at the time of the Assyrian conquest, had een transported from Galilee to Nineveh, where they lived precariously. But Tobit was able to remain obstinately faithful to the laws of Moses. At first things were not too bad. He became purveyor to the Assyrian king Enemesser and was able to save some money which he deposited with a distant relative in Media. But with the death of Enemesser he lost his job, and then got into trouble with the authorities for giving secret burial to Jews who had been murdered by Assyrians. As a result his property was confiscated, and on the top of all that he went blind. However, he had always given alms freely to fellow refugees and he continued to do so from his straitened resources – even when his wife had to take in piece-work for wages. She certainly lectured him on the precept that charity begins at home; and there was some unpleasantness when she brought home a kid which she said an employer had given her and he suspected her of having stolen it and told her to take it back. Tobit was reduced to tears, and prayed that he might die – but one can see Anna's point of view. There was more unpleasantness when he conceived the idea of sending young Tobias on this mad expedition to retrieve his money. It was then Anna's turn to be reduced to tears, because she was convinced that the boy would never come back alive. Why, oh why couldn't Tobit be content with what little they had? Was it not sufficient?

But Tobit was incurably – possibly exasperatingly – optimistic. Tobias would come back, he said. So, whether she believed it or not, Anna 'made an end of weeping', and Tobias set off with his dog and a rather mysterious hired servant, who appeared just at the right moment, and a long parting lecture from his father as to how he was to behave. But I think that Tobit had his doubts about seeing the boy again, because he added:

'My son, when I am dead, bury me; and despise not thy mother, but honour her all the days of thy life ... Remember, my son, that she saw many dangers for thee, when thou wast in her womb; and when she is dead, bury her by me in one grave.'

There were indeed some anxious moments during which Anna, fearing the worst, refused to eat and wailed at night. Indeed, Tobit must have had a difficult time with her. But his optimism was justified, because Tobias did come back, with the money and a delightful bride, and the servant, who then produced enough magic to restore Tobit's eyesight. And when they tried to reward him he disclosed himself as an archangel who had been sent by God to look after them – because of their good deeds.

'I am Raphael,' he said, 'one of the seven holy angels, which present the prayers of the saints, and which go in and out before the glory of the Holy One.'

Those who heard these words spoken by that gifted actor, Robert Eddison, in Bridie's play, will realize that seldom has a lovelier line been presented ready made to actor and playwright.

So Tobit and Anna lived happy ever after and were buried in one grave. And Tobit's optimism endured to the end; for though he foresaw the destruction of Jerusalem and the scattering of its people he also foresaw that:

'afterward they shall return from all places of their captivity, and build up Jerusalem gloriously, and the house of God shall be built in it for ever with a glorious building, as the prophets have spoken thereof. And all nations shall turn, and fear the Lord God truly, and shall bury their idols.'

Would to God we could bury some of ours!

A DISAPPOINTED REVIVALIST

These Old Testament stories are sometimes so vivid that I find it difficult not to see their personalities in terms of modern everyday life – particularly so in the case of Jonah. And I shall treat his, too, as a moral tale, though he is to be found among the minor prophets. I cannot help seeing him as a highly temperamental revivalist preacher in a black coat and a white necktie and enough sincerity to involve him in what we should now call an appalling guilt complex. The Lord had told him to conduct a mission in the wicked city of Nineveh, and for some reason he had funked it and gone off in the opposite direction with a tortured conscience. There followed his humiliating adventure inside a great fish. Our modern revivalist would doubtless say that he had been picked up by a submarine.

As for Nineveh it is easy to envisage it as a city full of gambling dens and strip-clubs and pornographic literature and drunkenness and municipal corruption – which it doubtless was, because that kind of wickedness doesn't seem to change much from age to age.

However, let us try to see Jonah in his middle eastern setting many centuries ago. He had been taught a lesson and he prayed to the Lord:

'The earth with her bars was about me for ever:
Yet hast thou brought up my life from corruption, O LORD my God.
When my soul fainted within me I remembered the LORD:
And my prayer came in unto thee, into thine holy temple.
They that observe lying vanities forsake their own mercy.
But I will sacrifice unto thee with the voice of thanksgiving;
I will pay that that I have vowed.'

And that he set out to do. He went to Nineveh and there conducted a successful mission. But in his own way. He threatened the city with destruction within forty days because of its wickedness and, that done, he made himself a little 'booth' well outside the city and sat waiting to see Nineveh share the fate of Sodom and Gomorrah – or Hiroshima and Nagasaki. What exactly would happen? In fact nothing did, because Jonah's preaching had been so effective that the citizens of Nineveh *did* repent, well and truly. They had a perfect orgy of repentance and the Lord's wrath was turned away and Nineveh was not destroyed after all.

One would suppose that Jonah would have been delighted with the success of his mission, but not at all. He had expected a spectacular event and when it didn't happen he was disappointed. He was worse than disappointed, he was very angry. He felt the Lord had let him down. He was angrier still when a gourd, which had afforded him some shade, died and the sun beat down on him. And on the top of that came what is described as a 'vehement east wind'. Well, anyone who knows the middle east knows that wind. It is called the *khamsin* and it sets everybody's nerves on edge. For Jonah it was the last straw and he said he wished he were dead. And then the Lord spoke to him and said, 'Doest thou well to be angry for the gourd?' And he said, 'I do well to be angry even unto death'. Which was no way to speak to the Lord. But the Lord was very patient with this hot, disappointed, nervy little prophet, and he said:

'Thou hast had pity on the gourd, for the which thou has not laboured, neither madest it grow; which came up in a night, and perished in a night: and should not I spare Nineveh, that great city, wherein are more than six score thousand persons that cannot discern between their right hand and their left hand; and also much cattle?'

Now here it seems to me that Jahweh, the God of Israel, is speaking with a new and yet familiar voice: the voice that centuries later was to record concern for two sparrows worth only a farthing, and to say, when surrounded by a mob of savage torturers:

'Father, forgive them; for they know not what they do'.

A DANIEL COME TO JUDGEMENT

I have always thought that Daniel, though by no means the greatest, is one of the most attractive characters of the Old Testament. So young; so gifted; and as I always imagine him, so debonair. He stood well with the Babylonian 'establishment' and was much respected after he had maintained his ground in the matter of ritual food and freedom of worship – and had indeed performed some brilliant feats of inspired soothsaying.

But it is in the Apocrypha that one of his most convincing exploits is related – I mean his rescue of Susanna by a very simple court procedure known to all magistrates today, namely the separate examination of witnesses out of hearing of one another to prevent collusion. Susanna was a Jewess, the wife of Joacim, a rich and much respected Jew. She was a religious young woman, well brought up in the law of Moses – and extremely pretty; which was nearly to prove her undoing! Joacim had a large enclosed garden; and one day when she was walking in it, she was observed by two elderly Babylonian judges – they are also described as elders. The sight of her inflamed their passions and filled their heads with lustful thoughts. At first they tried to conceal what was in their minds from one another; but when it became obvious that they were both bent on the same thing, they decided to act together. So they hid in the garden, which contained a bathing pool. When Susanna came down to bathe, having dismissed her maids – we are told that it was a hot day – they jumped out at her and made most improper suggestions, protesting that if she didn't yield to them they would accuse her of secret meetings in the garden with a fictitious young man.

Poor Susanna felt that she was in a trap. Either she had to face this shocking accusation – and she seems to have assumed that the elders would be believed (rightly, as it proved) – or she had to do something wholly foreign to her principles, her upbringing and her nature. She adopted the first alternative and the elders *were* believed. She was brought to trial and condemned to death on the charge that she had behaved improperly in the garden with a young man. The elders said that they had tried to catch the young man but had failed – which was not surprising, seeing that he didn't exist.

But at the last moment Daniel intervened. He insisted on reconstituting the court. He then separated the two elders and examined them separately. To the first he said, 'Under what tree did you see these two together?' 'Under a mastic tree,' the elder replied. Then the other elder was brought in and asked the same question. 'Under a holm tree,' he replied. With that the case against Susanna collapsed. It was clear the elders were lying. In the end it was they who suffered death for perjury. And Susanna's husband and parents and all her relatives were delighted to find that after all there was 'no dishonesty in her'.

But why did they ever suppose there was? The whole story seems to illustrate the eternal problem of possessive irrational sex-jealousy. I have seen that sort of thing when confronted with matrimonial disputes in a magistrate's court. Shakespeare knew all about it when he made Leontes in *The Winter's Tale* accept the flimsiest evidence of his wife's unfaithfulness. Indeed he convicted her on no evidence at all. Othello, of course, had more excuse. He was very cleverly framed and there was a colour complication which made him subconsciously unsure of himself as a husband.

But Joacim *knew* Susanna, knew what sort of a woman she was – everybody knew it. And yet he was ready to accept the uncorroborated evidence of two dirty-minded old men who weren't even fellow Jews. And anyway, what were these elderly judges doing – snooping round Susanna's bathing pool in her private garden? Nobody seems to have asked them that. Not even Daniel!

ELEAZAR AND THE PORK

Here is the story of Eleazar and the Pork. You will find it in Chapter Six of *The Second Book of the Maccabees* – part of the Old Testament Apocrypha. I imagine it happened some one hundred and fifty years before the birth of Christ, when the Jews were under Greek domination and attempts were being made to cajole and bully them out of their religious observances and make them pay respect to Bacchus and Jupiter. They were obviously having a dreadful time. Eleazar is described as 'one of the principal scribes, an aged man, and of a well favoured countenance'. And he seems to have been greatly venerated by the young. I always think of him as a sort of Gilbert Murray of his time. Perhaps that's why I have such an affection for him. But, as you will see, even his Greek persecutors were not wholly impervious to his charm. Well – here is what happened: so over to the account in the Apocrypha:

Eleazar . . . was constrained to open his mouth, and to eat swine's flesh. But he, choosing rather to die gloriously, than to live stained with such an abomination, spit it forth, and came of his own accord to the torment, as it behoved them to come, that are resolute to stand out against such things, as are not lawful for love of life to be tasted. But they that had the charge of that wicked feast, for the old acquaintance they had with the man, taking him aside, besought him to bring flesh of his own provision, such as was lawful for him to use, and make as if he did eat of the flesh taken from the sacrifice commanded by the king; that in so doing he might be delivered from death, and for the old friendship with them find favour.

But he began to consider discreetly, and as became his age, and the excellency of his ancient years, and the honour of his gray head, whereunto he was come, and his most honest education from a child, or rather the holy law made and given by God: therefore he answered accordingly, and willed them straightways to send him to the grave. 'For it becometh not our age', said he, 'in any wise to dissemble, whereby many young persons might think that Eleazar, being fourscore years old and ten, were now gone to a strange religion; and so they through mine hypocrisy, and desire to live a little time and a moment longer, should be deceived by me, and I get a stain to mine old age, and make it abominable . . . Wherefore now, man-

fully changing this life, I will show myself such an one as mine age re-
quireth, and leave a notable example to such as be young to die willingly
and courageously for the honourable and holy laws.' And when he had said
these words, immediately he went to the torment.

Now I think that's a grand story. It reflects such a profoundly
satisfying standard of values. What really mattered to Eleazar was
not the sin of eating pork which was forbidden to the Jews. He could
have avoided that with the friendly connivance of his captors. What
really mattered was whether he disillusioned his young people by
offering them the spectacle of an old scholarly man who allowed
himself to be bullied out of his principles. *That* was the sin he
wouldn't commit. Rather than commit that sin he was ready to face
an agonizing death. 'And thus', says the author of *The Second Book
of the Maccabees*, 'this man died, leaving his death for an example of
a noble courage, and a memorial of virtue, not only unto young men,
but unto all his nation.'

If you look in *The Listener*, 31 January 1957, you will find an
article by the Dean of St Paul's, Dr W. R. Matthews, about an old
scholarly Jew called Leo Baeck who had quite recently died after
having survived grievous bullying from the Germans. He must have
been very like Eleazar.

PERSIAN OIL

I'm going back again to *The Second Book of the Maccabees* to deal
with the affair of the Persian oil well. It is in Chapter One, and I
must confess that I can't find any religious significance in this story.
The fact is, when oil comes in at the door, religion flies out at the
window!

Now it seems that when the Jews were led away as exiles into
Persia, some of their priests took the holy fire of the altar – secretly –
and hid it in what is described as 'an hollow place of a pit without
water'. There they lay low. But when, years later, Nehemiah had
liberated his people from the Persians, he sent for those priests – or
rather their descendants. They explained that they had found in that
hollow what they described as 'no fire, but thick water'. Nehemiah
told them to fetch some of it along for one of their big religious

ceremonies, which they did. And now see what happened when the 'thick water' was poured on the altar:

When this was done, and the time came that the sun shone, which afore was hid in the cloud, there was a great fire kindled, so that every man marvelled.

It must have been a wonderful scene, and Nehemiah used the occasion to put up a very impressive prayer – as follows:

'O Lord, Lord God, Creator of all things, who art fearful and strong, and righteous, and merciful, and the only and gracious King, the only giver of all things, the only just, almighty, and everlasting, thou that deliverest Israel from all trouble, and didst choose the fathers, and sanctify them: receive the sacrifice for thy whole people Israel, and preserve thine own portion, and sanctify it. Gather those together that are scattered from us, deliver them that serve among the heathen, look upon them that are despised and abhorred, and let the heathen know that thou art our God. Punish them that oppress us, and with pride do us wrong. Plant thy people again in thy holy place, as Moses hath spoken.'

And when the prayer was finished there was a general thanksgiving. But mark the sequel – I'll give it to you as written:

When this matter was known, it was told the king of Persia, that in the place, where the priests that were led away had hid the fire, there appeared water, and that Nehemiah had purified the sacrifices therewith. Then the king, inclosing the place, made it holy, after he had tried the matter. And the king took many gifts, and bestowed thereof on those he would gratify. And Nehemiah called this thing Naphthar, which is as much as to say, a cleansing: but many men call it Nephi.

I must say, I like the King's choice of words! Having assured himself that the oil was really there, he 'inclosed the place, and made it holy'. In other words, he proclaimed a royal monopoly – and it seems to have been a profitable one.

Now as I have said, this cannot be described as a moral tale. I give it to you because I find it so interesting, and if others find it so and are thereby encouraged to read the Bible, that will be my excuse. But perhaps I may add that, like many another Bible story of dubious moral import, it tells us at any rate one thing about the baffling situations which face us in the modern world: many of them are not as new as we think. *Humanity has been there before.*

PART THREE

WISDOM

The Wisdom of Solomon, like *Maccabees*, is part of the Old Testament Apocrypha, and why it was accorded this semi-detached status in the Bible, I have never been able to understand. It is a kind of long philosophic poem and it contains some really lovely lines well able to bear comparison with *The Proverbs* and *Ecclesiastes*, the two 'wisdom' books of the canonical Old Testament.

THE WISDOM OF SOLOMON

In the thirteenth chapter of the book of *Wisdom* appears a fascinating comparison between the nature worshipper and the idol worshipper. The writer regards nature worship as perhaps understandable – but not enough. He hasn't a good word for the idolater. Well, here goes:

Surely vain are all men by nature, who are ignorant of God,
And could not out of the good things that are seen know him that is:
Neither by considering the works did they acknowledge the workmaster;
But deemed either fire, or wind, or the swift air,
Or the circle of the stars, or the violent water, or the lights of heaven
To be the gods which govern the world.
With whose beauty if they being delighted took them to be gods;
Let them know how much better the Lord of them is:
For the first author of beauty hath created them.
But if they were astonished at their power and virtue,
Let them understand by them, how much mightier he is that made them.
For by the greatness and beauty of the creatures
Proportionably the maker of them is seen.
But yet for this they are the less to be blamed:
For they peradventure err,
Seeking God, and desirous to find him . . .
Howbeit neither are they to be pardoned.
For if they were able to know so much,

That they could aim at the world,
How did they not sooner find out the Lord thereof?

And now for the idol worshippers:

But miserable are they, and in dead things is their hope,
Who called them gods, which are the works of men's hands,
Gold and silver, to shew art in, and resemblances of beasts,
Or a stone good for nothing, the work of an ancient hand.

There follows a vivid description of how an idol is made:

Now a carpenter that felleth timber, after he hath sawn down a tree meet
  for the purpose,
And taken off all the bark skilfully round about,
And hath wrought it handsomely, and made a vessel thereof fit for the
  service of man's life;
And after spending the refuse of his work to dress his meat, hath filled
  himself;
And taking the very refuse among those which served to no use,
Being a crooked piece of wood, and full of knots,
Hath carved it diligently, when he had nothing else to do,
And formed it by the skill of his understanding,
And fashioned it to the image of a man;
Or made it like some vile beast,
Laying it over with vermilion, and with paint colouring it red,
And covering every spot therein;
And when he had made a convenient room for it,
Set it in a wall, and made it fast with iron:
For he provided for it that it might not fall,
Knowing that it was unable to help itself;
For it is an image, and hath need of help:
Then maketh he prayer for his goods, for his wife and children,
And is not ashamed to speak to that which hath no life.

I'm inclined to think that our author – who is traditionally believed
to be King Solomon – is a little unfair to the idol maker. Because not
all idols are made of refuse material in somebody's spare time. Some
of them are made of beautiful material with great care. But the moral's
the same. They are all dead things. Whereas the man who appre-
hends divinity in the natural world is not very far from the kingdom
of heaven – perhaps half way there.

AN UNANSWERED QUESTION

In the book of *Wisdom* there is a passage which sets forth the viewpoint of the 'ungodly' with an indication that it is 'not aright'. 'Reasoning with themselves' they are credited with saying:

'Our life is short and tedious,
And in the death of a man there is no remedy . . .
For the breath of our nostrils is as smoke,
And a little spark in the moving of our heart:
Which being extinguished, our body shall be turned into ashes,
And our spirit shall vanish as the soft air,
And our name shall be forgotten in time . . .
Come on therefore, let us enjoy the good things that are present:
And let us speedily use the creatures like as in youth.
Let us fill ourselves with costly wine and ointments:
And let no flower of the spring pass by us:
Let us crown ourselves with rosebuds, before they be withered.'

Such moments of pessimism about life in general are not peculiar to the ungodly. Most of us experience them at times – and may be led to the conclusion that one might as well enjoy the good things that are present.

And indeed a very similar thought seems to have occurred to the writer of another book of the Old Testament – the book of *Ecclesiastes*, who was certainly not ungodly, though not altogether well regarded in some theological circles.

Looking out on life, he seems to have found that 'all was vanity and vexation of spirit'. He observed that a just man might perish and a wicked man prolong his life in his wickedness. He came to the conclusion that:

This is an evil among all things that are done under the sun, that there is one event unto all: yea, also the heart of the sons of men is full of evil, and madness is in their heart while they live, and after that they go to the dead. For to him that is joined to all the living there is hope: for a living dog is better than a dead lion. For the living know that they shall die: but the dead know not any thing, neither have they any more a reward; for the memory of them is forgotten. Also their love, and their hatred, and their envy, is now perished.

All this he felt and, worst of all, he felt that he couldn't find the answer. Why – why was life like this? He 'beheld that a man cannot find out the work that is done under the sun: because though a man labour to seek it out, yet he shall not find it'. That, I suspect, is a not uncommon experience in our day, as in his.

What then are we to do with this bankruptcy of human understanding? His advice, at first blush, is strangely reminiscent of those ungodly scaramouches in the book of *Wisdom*: 'Go thy way', he says, 'eat thy bread with joy and drink thy wine with a merry heart; for God now accepteth thy works. Let thy garments be always white; and let thy head lack no ointment. Live joyfully with the wife whom thou lovest all the days of thy vanity . . . : for that is thy portion in this life, and in thy labour which thou takest under the sun. Whatsoever thy hand findeth to do, do it with thy might'. And so, he says, 'It is good and comely for one to eat and to drink, and to enjoy the good of all his labour . . . for it is his portion . . . For he shall not much remember the *days* of his life; *because God answereth him in the joy of his heart.*' In fact he must live in the present and savour the fleeting moment, and find his answer to the mystery of why and wherefore, 'in the joy of his heart' as it responds to the good of his labour.

No such answer is offered to the ungodly in the book of *Wisdom*. They don't savour the fleeting moment, they clutch at it and gobble it. They may 'let no flower of the spring pass by them,' but I doubt if they have much feeling for flowers. They probably wire them to make bouquets, or pull their heads off to make festoons for royal receptions.

Perhaps that old heretic William Blake sums up the real difference in a poem entitled *Eternity*.

> He who bends to himself a joy
> Does the winged life destroy;
> But he who kisses the joy as it flies
> Lives in eternity's sunrise.

THE WISDOM OF THE AGES

I have called this series of talks 'The Unread Best-seller', because so many people have Bibles and so few people seem to read them. Now, thanks to retranslation and publication in a readable form, the New Testament seems to have justified the title 'best-seller' and, in addition, to have been read by a number of people who had got out of the habit of reading the old, familiar version. So perhaps I ought to have scrapped my title. Yet I fear it still holds good for the Old Testament. Here we have it still in its old form, unread perhaps, but written in magnificent Jacobean English. Let us make the best of it before it reappears in modern dress. It will look very strange. How, I wonder, will the retranslators render the phrase *Thus saith the Lord*? 'The Lord says'? We must wait and see.

The translators have got a difficult job – and nowhere more difficult than when they come to tackle the book called *The Wisdom of Solomon*, which contains so much of the wisdom of the ages, so much ageless human experience, and so many arresting phrases which are impossible to forget and sometimes difficult to understand. What for instance, can we make of this:

> Wickedness, condemned by her own witness, is very timorous,
> And being pressed with conscience, always forecasteth grievous things.
> For fear is nothing else but a betraying of the succours which reason offereth.

Whoever wrote *The Wisdom of Solomon* was well aware of the subjective torture of the human conscience, or what we might now call 'a guilt complex'. For see what goes on in the minds of the unrighteous:

> They being shut up in their houses, the prisoners of darkness,
> And fettered with the bonds of a long night,
> Lay there exiled from the eternal providence.
> For while they supposed to lie hid in their secret sins,
> They were scattered under a dark veil of forgetfulness,
> Being horribly astonished, and troubled with strange apparitions.

They couldn't sleep – they were 'shut up in a prison without iron bars'. It goes on:

> For they were all bound with one chain of darkness.
> Whether it were a whistling wind,
> Or a melodious noise of birds among the spreading branches,
> Or a pleasing fall of water running violently,

Or a terrible sound of stones cast down,
Or a running that could not be seen of skipping beasts,
Or a roaring voice of most savage wild beasts,
Or a rebounding echo from the hollow mountains;
These things made them swoon for fear.
For the whole world shined with a clear light,
And none were hindered in their labour:
Over them only was spread an heavy night,
An image of that darkness which should afterwards receive them.

But for those who escaped this hell of tortured conscience there was 'a very great light'. And nowhere, perhaps, do we find so splendid an expression of the spirit of divine love in the universe:

For the whole world before thee is as a little grain of the balance,
Yea, as a drop of the morning dew that falleth down upon the earth.
But thou hast mercy upon all; for thou canst do all things,
And winkest at the sins of men, because they should amend.
For thou lovest all things that are,
And abhorrest nothing which thou hast made:
For never wouldest thou have made any thing, if thou hadst hated it.
And how could any thing have endured, if it had not been thy will?
Or been preserved, if not called by thee?
But thou sparest all: for they are thine,
O Lord, thou lover of souls.

But *Wisdom* contains a word of warning – more relevant and more menacing to us today than ever before in the long history of mankind –

Pull not upon yourselves destruction with the works of your hands.

Has mankind ever got so near to doing that as it is today?

THE WISDOM OF JESUS BEN SIRACH

Jesus is a name which means only one person to Christians, but it was a very common name in ancient Israel; and the Jesus I am going to talk about is an earlier Jesus who wrote some time about the year 180 B.C. A nameless editor, writing perhaps fifty years later, says: 'This Jesus was the son of Sirach, and grandchild to Jesus of the same name with him: this man therefore lived in the latter times, after the people had been led away captive, and called home again, and almost after all the prophets'. His grandfather Jesus had, it seems, begun to collect wise sayings, adding some of his own. But he left his work unfinished and Sirach his son handed it on to grandson Jesus who, our unknown editor says, 'compiled it all orderly into one volume, and called it Wisdom'. We know it as *Ecclesiasticus*, but it is in fact a book of profound wisdom, not unmixed with shrewd common sense, and very much alive in the twentieth century. Even when it comes to economic affairs and the status of manual workers. Here, indeed, Jesus ben Sirach seems to have anticipated Karl Marx in diagnosing a fundamental class struggle:

> What fellowship hath the wolf with the lamb?
> So the sinner with the godly.
> What agreement is there between the hyena and a dog?
> And what peace between the rich and the poor?
> As the wild ass is the lion's prey in the wilderness:
> So the rich eat up the poor.

And how comes this class cleavage? Surely, as he points out elsewhere, in the denial of leisure and learning to the workers: the smith, who 'fighteth with the heat of the furnace: the noise of the hammer and the anvil is ever in his ears'; the potter at his wheel; the carpenter, 'that laboureth night and day'. 'And how,' he asks, 'can he get wisdom that holdeth the plough?' Admittedly these men 'will maintain the state of the world', and 'without these cannot a city be inhabited'. Nevertheless:

> They shall not dwell where they will, nor go up and down:
> They shall not be sought for in publick counsel,
> Nor sit high in the congregation:
> They shall not sit on the judges' seat,
> Nor understand the sentence of judgment.

Now someone else said very much the same thing, speaking to manual workers some two thousand years later. He said:

'You may become strong and clamorous, you may win a victory, you may effect a revolution, but you will be trodden down again under the feet of knowledge unless you get it for yourselves ... you will be trodden down again if you leave knowledge in the hands of privilege, because knowledge will always win over ignorance.'

Who said that? Karl Marx? No, Charles Gore, Bishop of Birmingham, speaking in the Wesleyan Central Hall at Sheffield to members of the Workers' Educational Association in the year 1909. But here in England, thanks to much that has happened since 1909, Jesus ben Sirach is a little out of date because now the workers do 'sit high in the congregation' and are 'sought for in public counsel'.

And some may think that in his views of parental discipline ben Sirach has fallen a little behind our times, though personally I am not so sure. He did, of course, believe strongly in discipline and even corporal punishment for the young. But as regards treatment of parents he can still inspire us:

> My son, help thy father in his age,
> And grieve him not as long as he liveth.
> And if his understanding fail, have patience with him.

What he says about fathers clearly relates also to mothers, to whom he accords full parental status – except in one much-quoted passage which will be the subject of my next chapter. As a matter of fact, mothers have even more need of such patience since they live longer – and grow older, and at any given moment there are more of them.

HEBREW HEROES IN RETROSPECT

There is one chapter in the Apocrypha which is probably better known than almost any chapter of the Old Testament, because of the passage in it which is read again and again at Founder's Day celebrations in schools and colleges. I won't read it now because it is already so familiar. It begins, 'Let us now praise famous men, and our fathers that begat us.' It is a lovely passage – though I always think it is a little unfair on the mothers that bore us – a much more troublesome and tedious process! But that's by the way. It finishes up with the immortal lines:

> Their bodies are buried in peace;
> But their name liveth for evermore.
> The people will tell of their wisdom,
> And the congregation will shew forth their praise.

And there the Founder's Day reading ends. But if you turn up the chapter – it is *Ecclesiasticus Forty-four* – you will find that this passage is just the introduction to a series of – what shall we call them? – poetic thumb-nail sketches of the great men of Hebrew history. It begins with Enoch, who 'pleased the Lord, and was translated, being an example of repentance to all generations'. And ends with Simon the high priest, who repaired the temple, improved the water supply and fortified Jerusalem... He must have been a blazing personality for:

> In his coming out of the sanctuary
> He was as the morning star in the midst of a cloud,
> And as the moon at the full:
> As the sun shining upon the temple of the Most High,
> And as the rainbow giving light in the bright clouds:
> And as the flower of roses in the spring of the year.

Dear me, of how many public dignitaries could one say that?
But in fact the whole series is full of these rich lyrical outbursts. For instance, the prophet Elijah:

> Then stood up Elias the prophet as fire,
> And his word burned like a lamp.

However, it's not literary richness I want to call your attention to, but the standard of spiritual values that runs through the whole series.

Moses is remembered as 'a merciful man, which found favour in the sight of all flesh'. He is remembered, not as the national liberator who tricked the Egyptians, but as the man to whom God showed 'part of his glory' – and who was thus sanctified 'in his faithfulness and meekness' and who brought 'the law of life and knowledge' to Israel.

Samuel certainly did some valiant work against the Philistines – which is noted – but:

> Before his long sleep he made protestations in the sight of the Lord and
> his anointed,
> 'I have not taken any man's goods, so much as a shoe':
> And no man did accuse him.

But the picture I like best is that of King David. His spectacular affair with Goliath is duly recorded – he is after all the great hero of Hebrew history – perhaps the greatest. But what is stressed here is the fact that he brought aesthetic beauty into worship. I know that some people doubt whether it should be brought in, on the ground that it is irrelevant and distracting. But the author of *Ecclesiasticus* didn't think so, for he says of David:

In all his works he praised the Holy One Most High with words of glory;
With his whole heart he sung songs,
And loved him that made him,
He set singers also before the altar,
That by their voices they might make sweet melody,
And daily sing praises in their songs.
He beautified their feasts,
And set in order the solemn times until the end,
That they might praise his holy name,
And that the temple might sound from morning.
The Lord took away his sins,
And exalted his horn for ever:
He gave him a covenant of kings,
And a throne of glory in Israel.

He did a lot of bad things and I always think it is surprisingly honest of Hebrew historians to record them of their great hero. But he was not only a hero. He was a musician and a poet.

POSTSCRIPT

I suppose that, apart from *Ecclesiasticus Forty-four*, the Apocrypha is the least read part of the Old Testament. In fact a great many Bibles don't contain it, which is a pity because some of the most enthralling history (*Maccabees*, for instance) and some of the profoundest thought (*Wisdom*, for instance) is in it. But there's one part of the Apocrypha which I have never been able to understand, and that is *The Second Book of Esdras*. And when I found a large volume devoted to the subject of Esdras II, I still couldn't make head or tail of it. Who *was* Esdras II? Nobody seems to know. When did he live? Nobody seems to know. Anyway, as you read this strange, obscure, apocryphal book, the personality of Esdras II emerges, and you find him on page after page in hot argument with the archangel Uriel about what we might call the logic of history or, perhaps even, the meaning of life.

Esdras asks questions; the archangel, as representing the Lord, replies to them. Esdras is never wholly satisfied; the archangel, to my mind, never wholly clear. And Esdras asks the kind of questions we ask today   that mankind will doubtless go on asking to the end of time.

Esdras is a Jew, and a Jew writing of his people beaten, scattered and in exile. Why are they like this? he asks. Yes, of course, they have transgressed, and that in spite of all that the Lord has done for them. But, says Esdras:

'Are their deeds any better that inhabit Babylon, that they should therefore have the dominion over Sion? ... For I have seen how thou sufferest them sinning, and hast spared wicked doers: and hast destroyed thy people, and hast preserved thine enemies, and hast not signified unto any how thy way may be comprehended: are they then of Babylon better than they of Sion?'

To Esdras it doesn't seem to make sense. The evil prosper, the good (the comparatively good) come to grief. At one point the archangel suggests that Esdras wants to know too much. 'Thy heart hath gone too far in this world,' he says, 'and thinkest thou to

71

comprehend the way of the Most High?' To which Esdras replies, 'Yea, my Lord'. So the archangel comes back at him and asks him whether he can weigh the weight of the fire, or measure the blast of the wind, or call back again the day that is past. And Esdras has to admit that he can't; at which the archangel twits him with, 'Thine own things and such as are grown up with thee canst thou not know; how should thy vessel then be able to comprehend the way of the Highest?' And Esdras says, 'It were better that we were not at all, than that we should live still in wickedness, and to suffer, and not to know wherefore'. And so it goes on hammer and tongs night after night, with long periods of fasting for Esdras in between the bouts. And I get the impression that Esdras never got to the bottom of the matter, as many of us fail to do today. But at least he knew that the Lord was prepared to let him argue it out; so in the end he put up a grand prayer:

'O Lord, thou that dwellest in everlastingness, which beholdest from above things in the heaven and in the air; whose throne is inestimable; whose glory may not be comprehended; before whom the hosts of angels stand with trembling, (whose service is conversant in wind and fire,) whose word is true, and sayings constant; whose commandment is strong, and ordinance fearful; whose look drieth up the depths, and indignation maketh the mountains to melt away ... O hear the prayer of thy servant, and give ear to the petition of thy creature. For while I live I will speak, and so long as I have understanding I will answer ...'

There is one thing certain about this obscure prophet, Esdras II. He knew the meaning of the word which is spelled *awe*. He knew that it was the first condition of worship. He also knew, from his encounter with the archangel, that the Lord is tolerant of argument and not disposed to confuse doubt with blasphemy. So even the most argumentative amongst us can 'lift up our hearts' with Esdras II.